Also available at all good book stores

9781785315466

9781785313929

9781785316470

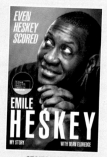

9781785315008

9781785315534

9781785317224

ON THIS DAY

HISTORY, FACTS AND FIGURES
FROM EVERY DAY OF THE YEAR

ROB BURNETT & JOE MEWIS

ENGLAND
ON THIS DAY
HISTORY, FACTS AND FIGURES
FROM EVERY DAY OF THE YEAR

All statistics, facts and figures are correct as of 1st September 2009;
and updated 2020

© Rob Burnett and Joe Mewis

Rob Burnett and Joe Mewis have asserted their rights in accordance with the Copyright,
Designs and Patents Act 1988 to be identified as the authors of this work.

Published By:
Pitch Publishing (Brighton) Ltd
A2 Yeoman Gate
Yeoman Way
Durrington
BN13 3QZ

Email: info@pitchpublishing.co.uk
Web: www.pitchpublishing.co.uk

First published 2009; reprinted and updated 2020

A catalogue record for this book is available from the British Library.

13-digit ISBN: 978 1 78531 719 4

Printed and bound in Great Britain by TJ Books Limited

INTRODUCTION

Welcome to *England On This Day*, a history of the England team that, as the cliché goes, takes it one day at a time.

Following England in recent years has been a stressful mix of incompetent managers, broken metatarsals, penalty shoot-outs, the 'left-sided problem' and a team that's less than the sum of its parts – punctuated by the occasional joyous run to the semi-finals of a major tournament – as the 1966 triumph disappears further and further into the sunset.

It wasn't always this way though. For the first 50 years of their existence the England team was, give or take the odd challenge from Scotland, the best in the world.

Since then the rest of the world has wised up, often leaving the Three Lions lagging behind, but this hasn't stopped England having one of the most fanatical followings on the planet.

Contained within these pages are England's greatest victories, most spectacular goals, biggest personalities and record breakers. Oh, and a couple of shoot-out losses to the Germans.

Some you'll remember, some you'll wish you did and others you'll have tried to forget, but here are all the stories that make being an England fan that unique mix of pride, passion and disappointment that somehow always keeps us coming back for more.

Rob Burnett and Joe Mewis

ACKNOWLEDGEMENTS

First and foremost, thanks to Joe, who took on the lion's share of work for this book, particularly the research. Without him putting in extra work, this project would never have been finished on time. Thanks as ever to Bard and Annemarie for their help and support, and to Emily, for whom patience does not come easily yet who has somehow learned how to harness it while I was writing this book.

Rob Burnett

Thanks to Paul Camillin and all those at Pitch and to family, friends and colleagues that have supported and helped us on the way. For England-based inspiration, thanks to the Germany '06 campervan crew: Tom Butterworth, Mark Corr, Stuart Meney and for the torrent of social networking-based suggestions: Howard Lancaster and Mike 'Creed' Corr. Finally, without being too cheesy, thanks to Rob for all the hard work over the last few months.

Joe Mewis

ENGLAND
ON THIS DAY

JANUARY

JANUARY 1

England legend Stanley Matthews became the first footballer to be awarded a Knighthood today in 1965 when the Queen honoured the Wizard of the Dribble for his 33 years of service on the football pitch. Incredibly enough, Matthews, one month short of his 50th birthday, was still playing top-flight football for Stoke City and would have broken all manner of England records had it not been for the outbreak of World War II and the suspension of international football.

Also receiving a gong from Her Maj in the New Year's Honours list was Gary Lineker who picked up an OBE today in 1992. Everyone's favourite crisp eater celebrated by scoring in Tottenham's 2-1 win over Coventry City later that day.

JANUARY 2

Manchester United were doing their bit to help out the FA in their bid for the 2006 World Cup today in 2000 as they arrived in Rio de Janeiro for the World Club Challenge. After much political pressure from Fifa, the FA and even the government, United pulled out of that season's FA Cup to travel to Brazil, where they crashed out in the group stage and were accused of devaluing the world's oldest cup competition in the process. With England's 2006 bid failing, the whole exercise was about as redundant as a stockroom full of Cristiano Ronaldo shirts at Old Trafford.

Another former United player that made headlines in South America was Charlie Mitten, who died today in 2002. Mitten only played one game for England, an unofficial charity match against Scotland at Maine Road in 1946, but was more famous for being one of the so-called 'Bogotá Bandits' that succumbed to the big bucks of a group of wealthy Colombian businessmen that were intent on bringing big names to the Colombian league. He would later go on to manage Mansfield Town and Newcastle United.

JANUARY 3

Sepp Blatter, the man it was once said 'has 50 new ideas every day and 51 of them are bad' came up with another gem today in 1999 when he said the World Cup should become biennial. 'The existing four-yearly tournament is out of date,' he rambled. 'It dates from the 1930s when teams chugged from one continent to another on ships.' Thankfully his suggestions were laughed out of town, as watching England crash out on penalties once every four years is quite enough Mr Blatter.

Since breaking onto the scene at the World Cup in 1998, Michael Owen has had enough injuries to fill this book on his own. Today in 2006 he was going under the knife to repair the foot that England teammate Paul Robinson had broken when Owen's Newcastle took on Tottenham four days earlier. Optimists believed this meant Owen would return in time for that summer's World Cup as fresh as a daisy, but he instead looked every inch the player who hadn't played for half a season in Germany later that year.

JANUARY 4

Howard Wilkinson was entrusted with nurturing the next generation of England stars today in 1997, when he was offered the post of FA technical director. The recently departed Leeds manager remained in the post until joining Sunderland in 2002, where he managed only two wins in 20 games before being sacked.

John Terry's emergence in the England team was put under threat today in 2002, when the Chelsea youngster was charged with assault and affray after a night out in London with club teammate Jody Morris and Wimbledon defender Desmond Byrne. Terry would later be cleared of all charges, but was handed a temporary England ban by the FA. This came only months after Terry had been fined two weeks' wages by Chelsea after drunkenly harassing American tourists at a Heathrow hotel in the immediate aftermath of the September 11th attacks in 2001.

JANUARY 5

Bobby Moore opened his England goalscoring account today in 1966 when he bagged England's equaliser in a 1-1 draw with Poland at Anfield. This didn't really mark the start of a great goalscoring run for the England skipper as he only scored one more goal, but his two strikes in 108 appearances is only a marginally worse ratio than Emile Heskey's.

Other than scoring goals and wearing his heart on his sleeve, Kevin Keegan did what he does best today in 1997, quitting the Newcastle manager's job. The former England captain gave England fans a preview of things to come, although he saved his resignation for the boardroom, not the St James' toilets.

JANUARY 6

He'd picked up the World Cup with England, the FA Cup and Cup Winners' Cup with West Ham and was closing in on 100 England caps, but today in 1971 Bobby Moore was given the ultimate television honour, when he was presented with the big red book on *This Is Your Life*.

If the arcane England Selection Committee had relinquished their powers earlier and appointed an England manager before Walter Winterbottom in 1946, then they would have surely given the job to Herbert Chapman, the revolutionary Huddersfield Town and Arsenal manager that died today in 1934 after catching pneumonia watching an Arsenal third team take on Guildford City. Chapman was the great moderniser of his era, introducing a host of new tactics and training methods to the English game, championing innovations such as floodlighting, numbered shirts and European club competitions. He was also hit with a ban from the game by the FA when he was Leeds City manager, during the illegal payments scandal that forced the club out of existence.

JANUARY 7

After a disastrous experiment with a home-grown manager, England went back to going overseas for their new boss, as Fabio Capello took over the post today in 2008. The former Milan, Real Madrid and Juventus coach came with one of the best CVs in the game, having won six Serie A, two La Liga and one Champions League title, but was a rookie on the international stage. The move was warmly met by England fans' figurehead Mark Perryman, who said: 'It's like replacing Captain Mainwaring with Field-Marshal Montgomery.'

When Capello was in charge of Real Madrid he lashed out at David Beckham's decision to move to LA Galaxy and he undoubtedly had the England manager's voice in his head when he decided to temporarily ditch the MLS, joining AC Milan on loan for the rest of the season today in 2009.

JANUARY 8

The winter of 1962-63 was extremely harsh, with Blackpool not being able to play a single home game between December 15 and March 2 due to their pitch at Bloomfield Road being completely frozen. Today in 1963 Seasiders' England right-back Jimmy Armfield and teammate Tony Waiters saw this a chance to take up ice skating, taking to the pitch to practise their double axels and triple loops.

Today in 1994 Glenn Hoddle was taking charge of his first FA Cup match as Chelsea player-manager and the soon-to-be England boss found himself up against an unlikely opponent: his younger brother Carl who played for the Blues' opposition Barnet. Hoddle junior was on the books with Glenn at Spurs but failed to make the grade and when the two met on the pitch he mixed bossing the Barnet midfield with running a pub. The Bees held their cross-city rivals to a 0-0 draw at Underhill, but Chelsea won the replay 4-0 at Stamford Bridge.

JANUARY 9

Two months earlier Sven-Göran Eriksson had agreed to take over as England boss at the end of the 2000/01 season, but today in 2001 the Lazio boss decided not to bother hanging around and quit the Rome club to take charge of the Three Lions – and the handsomely paid contract that came with it – six months ahead of schedule. The Swede took to the pitch at the Olympic Stadium at the end of Lazio's friendly with China shedding a tear or two as he told the fans he was leaving. They responded with a banner reading: 'Goodbye Mister Eriksson, you are a champion of style.'

England captain John Terry was in the headlines for the wrong reasons again today in 2007, as he was fined £10,000 for improper conduct after slating referee Graham Poll. Serial ref-botherer Terry claimed in the media that Poll had given him conflicting reasons for sending him off against Tottenham two months earlier.

JANUARY 10

Terry Venables announced today in 1996 that he would be leaving the England job after the summer's forthcoming European Championships. El Tel hadn't been offered a top club job or anything respectable like that, but decided he needed to concentrate full-time on the growing number of murky and boring court cases that his failing business career appeared to be throwing up.

One of Sven-Göran Eriksson's first moves as England manager was to bring in his trusty number two, Tord Grip, and it only took 12 months for the pressure of the toughest job in football to show, as Grip was admitted to hospital with a heart problem today in 2002. Grip was quickly released from hospital but had to call off a trip to the African Nations Cup.

JANUARY 11

David Beckham shocked the footballing world by announcing today in 2007 that he would be leaving Real Madrid at the end of the season to join MLS side LA Galaxy. The former England skipper said he was looking to raise the sport's profile in America and would be receiving a reported £128m over five years for his troubles. Madrid boss Fabio Capello was furious at the decision, saying Beckham would never play for Real again, before making a u-turn and reinstalling him in the side as Los Merengues went on to win the La Liga title.

Following Terry Venables' announcement that he would be standing down as England boss after the European Championships, Kevin Keegan told the FA he was 'not interested' in leaving Newcastle to take up the vacant post today in 1996.

JANUARY 12

England officially appointed their first-ever foreign manager today in 2001 when the FA handed the reins of football's toughest job to Sven-Göran Eriksson. 'If we don't get results, they will try to hang me. But if I was an Englishman they would try to hang me,' joked the Swede at his unveiling at FA headquarters. Five years of womanising, substitute-tastic friendlies, broken metatarsals and quarter-final exits beckoned.

English football was in mourning on this day in 2017 for one of Sven's predecessors, Graham Taylor, who had died aged 72. It is a sad truth that Taylor was more well known for his unsuccessful spell as England boss – captured so brilliantly in the documentary *An Impossible Job* – than he was for his incredible club football achievements, mostly with Watford and Aston Villa. There was only one thing to say when this news broke: 'Do I not like that.'

JANUARY 13

Today in 1997, fresh from the success of Euro 96, the FA launched an ill-fated bid to host the 2006 World Cup. Starting as favourites, it looked good for England until Sepp Blatter spoke of his desire to bring the tournament to Africa and then the Germans got in on the act, soon becoming front-runners. When England fans rioted at the 1998 World Cup in France and again two years later in the European Championships any hopes of bringing the world's biggest sporting competition to England had gone up in smoke.

A shoulder injury forced one of England's greatest-ever goalkeepers to quit the game today in 2004. Although he had his fair share of high-profile gaffes between the posts, David Seaman racked up 75 caps, making him England's second-most capped 'keeper, behind Peter Shilton. Man City quickly moved to replace Safehands with his successor in the England goal, David James.

JANUARY 14

England welcomed Johan Cruyff and his total-footballing Dutch side to Wembley today in 1970. Cruyff was beginning to re-establish himself in the Oranje side after being sent off against Czechoslovakia in his second game and receiving a year-long ban from the Dutch FA, but could not inspire his teammates, as the two countries played out a 0-0 draw in front of 75,000 fans. Bobby Charlton thought he'd given England a win at the death when he hit the back of the net, but the final whistle had already gone.

When 16-year-old Theo Walcott turned out for Southampton against QPR in the Championship clash today in 2006, few believed that this would be his last league game before making his England debut ahead of that summer's World Cup. Walcott's £9m move to Arsenal went through days after Saints' 1-0 loss to the Rs and he would go on to be the wild card in Sven's World Cup squad.

STEVE BLOOMER, ENGLAND'S FIRST SUPERSTAR

JANUARY 15

Sven-Göran Eriksson had a nasty surprise when he went to pick up the Sunday papers today in 2006 and found that his new wealthy best pal with whom he had spilled the beans with regard to his England players and future plans was none-other than undercover *News of the World* reporter Mazher Mahmood, or the 'fake sheikh' as he is better known. After saying he would be interested in taking over at Aston Villa following that summer's World Cup, that Rio Ferdinand was lazy and Wayne Rooney came from a poor family, Sven described the stunt as 'a kick under the belt' and commenced legal proceedings, but the writing was on the wall for his England career.

It's hard to imagine Sir Alf ever sharing a yacht with Arabian royalty. Today in 1969 Ramsey was where he was most comfortable, on the Wembley sideline, as his side struggled to a 1-1 draw with Romania. Jack Charlton's opening goal was cancelled out by Florea Dumitrache's second-half penalty.

JANUARY 16

England eagerly awaited today's draw for the forthcoming World Cup in 1982, having not played in the competition since Gerd Müller and West Germany had dumped them out of the 1970 tournament in Mexico. What happened next was a textbook Fifa balls-up, as the draw-masters initially forgot to separate the seeded teams and then the containers holding the balls jammed, splitting open and cascading ping-pong balls everywhere. The farce was compounded when West German representative Hermann Neuberger accused the organisers of slave labour by using Spanish orphans to fetch the balls back and forth.

Fabio Capello had only been in the England job for ten days when it was announced that he was under investigation for alleged tax evasion in Italy. This made a change from Sven's wrongdoings that usually involved tabloid kiss and tells but no charges have since been brought against the Italian.

JANUARY 17

England took on Scotland in a wartime international today in 1942, with the Three Lions winning 3-0 thanks to a brace from Tommy Lawton and a goal from James Hagan. The blitz spirit was in full effect as over 64,000 fans turned up for the match at Wembley. Whilst these contests were not recognised by Fifa as official internationals, the British government believed it vital for morale to keep the nation's favourite pastime going, with Winston Churchill turning up to a match in October 1941.

Lord knows what Churchill would have made of Gazza's antics today in 1994 when a photo of the Lazio and England playmaker appeared on the front of Italian newspaper *Il Messaggero* with his manhood flopping out of his shorts, taken during a match against Foggia. Both Lazio and the newspaper received a deluge of calls from angry Romans and the paper gave the old 'it's an optical illusion' excuse.

JANUARY 18

After seven matches against the Scots, England got a new opponent today in 1879, when they played Wales for the first time. The Welsh had played and lost against Scotland three times before they went to the Oval to play England. With a blizzard coming down the match was shortened to two 30-minute halves and reports say that only between 85 and 300 attended due to the poor conditions. England were forced to start with only ten men as William Clegg turned up 20 minutes late, but by the time Clegg was up and running England were a goal up thanks to Herbert Whitfield. Thomas Heathcote Sorby of Thursday Wanderers scored a second on his only cap before William H Davies pulled one back for the Welsh who battled to a respectable 2-1 defeat.

England have met Wales 101 times since and another team they are sick of the sight of is Poland, their 1973 nemesis. Today in 1998 England were drawn in the same Euro 2000 qualifying group as the Poles, for the fifth consecutive time in a major tournament qualifying competition.

England On This Day

JANUARY 19

With operations at Fifa still suspended following the Second World War, England played an unofficial game against Belgium at Wembley today in 1946. Dubbed a 'victory international', England won 2-0 with first-half strikes from Charlton's Robert Brown and Jesse Pye of Notts County in front of a crowd of 85,000.

As well as going down in history as West Brom's favourite-ever player Jeff Astle won over a new generation of fans on Baddiel and Skinner's *Fantasy Football League*, where the former England striker and staple of the 1970 World Cup anthem *Back Home* would serenade the crowd with a song over the credits. Astle, nicknamed 'The King', died today in 2002 from a brain disease that was caused by the repeated minor trauma of heading old-fashioned leather footballs.

JANUARY 20

One of England's forgotten greats was born today in 1874. Steve Bloomer made 23 appearances for England at the turn of the century, racking up 28 goals to become the nation's leading scorer. Domestically, he plied his trade up front for Derby County and Middlesbrough, scoring 317 goals in 536 league games and after retiring he went to coach in Germany, but weeks later World War I broke out and he found himself in a prisoner of war camp, where he helped organise football and cricket games before being liberated in 1918. He then went to coach in the Netherlands and finally Spain, where he guided Real Union to the Spanish title.

Today in 2004 Rio Ferdinand began his eight-month ban for missing a drugs test the previous September. Ferdinand had told the FA he had forgotten to take the test as he was moving house and had to go shopping, but this didn't wash and he was hit with a £50,000 fine as well as being forced to sit out England's Euro 2004 challenge.

JANUARY 21

Having seen Scotland go four years without beating England, Bolton outside-forward Alex Donaldson was obviously of the belief that 'if you can't beat them, join them', when he headed up to Sunderland today in 1914 for an England international trial game and tried to blag a place in the Three Lions' side. Just before kick-off he 'fessed up and played for the Scots in their 3-1 win over England three months later in the final England match before the outbreak of the First World War.

Today in 1973 England took on Wales in a World Cup qualifier at Wembley, drawing 1-1. Future Wales boss John Toshack opened the scoring, but the Dragons were soon pegged back by a Norman Hunter strike just before half-time.

JANUARY 22

Sir Alf Ramsey, the only man to succeed where every other England manager has so far failed, was born in Dagenham today in 1920. Sir Alf came from a working class background and played for Portsmouth in the London War League before moving to Southampton to begin his professional career in 1943, where he built up a reputation as an excellent reader of the game, turning out at right-back for England on 32 occasions. Nicknamed 'the General', Ramsey moved into management with Ipswich after hanging up his boots, where his exploits alerted him to the FA, who appointed him in 1963.

Sir Alf shared his birthday with another England great, Everton striker Dixie Dean, who was born today in 1907. Dean bagged a remarkable 12 goals in his first five games for England and was a renowned hard man, going under the knife 15 times during his career and after having a metal plate inserted in his skull following a motorcycle crash. He was back on the pitch within three months.

JANUARY 23

After being suckered by the 'fake sheikh' a week earlier, Sven-Göran Eriksson announced today in 2006 that he would be stepping down as England manager after the 2006 World Cup. Sven was quick to allay fears his heart might not be in it during England's travails in Germany that summer by saying: 'It is important to stress how committed I am to success this summer. Let's go and win the World Cup.' This battle cry was nowhere near enough to catapult England to World Cup glory, but with a reported £3m compensation package it's unlikely that the Swede was crying into his P45.

An 18-year-old Jermain Defoe got England fans' pulses a-racing today in 2001, as he broke the post-war record of goals in consecutive games, making it ten in a row when the on-loan striker scored for Bournemouth against Cambridge. Plenty of 'England's next big thing' type headlines appeared, and Defoe ended his England career with 20 goals in 57 appearances.

JANUARY 24

Prolific Notts County goalscorer Jackie Sewell was born today in 1927. The inside-forward made six appearances for England, scoring three times, but saw his international career go up in smoke when he was part of the two England teams that were humbled by the Mighty Magyars of Hungary in 1953 and 1954. After scoring 97 times in 179 games for the Magpies Sewell was transferred to Sheffield Wednesday for an English record £34,500 in 1951.

Five years earlier Stoke City's Cornelius 'Neil' Franklin, one of the so-called 'Bogotá Bandits' was born. Franklin had represented England 27 times when he broke his contract at the Victoria Ground to join Independiente Santa Fe on a £5,000-per year contact, with a £35 win bonus on top. However, after only four weeks in Colombia he returned after political and social unrest made it hard for Franklin and his family to settle. A ban from the England team awaited him on his return.

JANUARY 25

The draw was made for the Euro 2004 qualifying campaign today in 2002 and England were handed a diplomatic and security headache when they were paired with Turkey. This came only two years after two Leeds fans had been killed prior to their Uefa Cup tie with Galatasaray and further clashes between fans when the Istanbul club took on Arsenal in the final later that season. Making up the numbers in group seven was the undaunting trio of Slovakia, FYR Macedonia and Liechtenstein.

Trevor Sinclair was filling England's infamous 'problem left hand side' at this time and today in 1997 he scored his most famous goal: a spectacular overhead kick for QPR against Barnsley in the FA Cup that bagged him *Match of the Day*'s goal of the season.

JANUARY 26

Today in 2006 the FA announced they wanted to appoint Sven's successor before the World Cup got underway in Germany that summer. A three-man team were dispatched to sound out candidates, coming up with a shortlist including Martin O'Neill, Guus Hiddink, Alan Curbishley, Stuart Pearce and Sam Allardyce. Somehow, Steve McClaren also sneaked onto the radar.

One of the best managers that England never had was Tottenham stalwart Bill Nicholson, who was born today in 1919. As a player Nicholson turned out at wing-half 314 times for Spurs and was a one-cap wonder with the England team, but as manager led Spurs to English football's first double of the twentieth century in 1961. He also chipped in during the 1958 World Cup, assisting manager Walter Winterbottom in Sweden.

JANUARY 27

Today in 2006 out-going England manager Sven-Göran Eriksson reacted to the draw for the Euro 2008 qualifying campaign, sounding every bit the man that knew he would not be in charge when it started. 'I think it's a good draw,' he said. 'I think England should be happy with that draw. I'm convinced they will pass through rather easily. He should be happy with the draw and he will be, whoever it is.' His former assistant Steve McClaren would not have wanted to be reminded of these words two years later when he had made a pig's ear of what Sven saw as a silk purse.

Former England international Gary Charles, the man most famous for being on the receiving end of Paul Gascoigne's infamous knee-high tackle in the 1991 FA Cup Final, appeared in court today in 2003 after ploughing his car into a garden wall and being found in a drunken stupor. Injuries had forced an early end to his playing career and he was jailed in December 2006 after committing a public order offence whilst serving a suspended sentence.

JANUARY 28

Wheeler-dealer Terry Venables blagged himself the England manager job today in 1994. The former Tottenham gaffer left White Hart Lane after falling out with Spurs chairman Alan Sugar and stayed in the England job for two-and-a-half years, leading the Three Lions to Euro 96 before becoming the first England manager to resign from the post for dodgy business dealings.

Venables had a three-year spell as Barcelona boss that saw him pick up the nickname 'El Tel' and today in 1999 Steve McManaman was dubbed 'El Macca' as the England and Liverpool midfielder agreed to join Real Madrid on a Bosman transfer at the end of the season. The Scouser was an instant hit with the Bernabéu faithful, scoring a spectacular volley in the 2000 Champions League final as he picked up a pair of La Liga and European Cup titles.

JANUARY 29

Bobby Robson handed debuts to Southampton winger Danny Wallace and Liverpool striker Peter Beardsley for a friendly against Egypt in Cairo today in 1986. England saw off the Pharaohs 4-0, with Trevor Steven scoring England's 1,500th goal in the process. Wallace marked his debut with a goal, but this would be his only international appearance and his career would later be cut short when he was diagnosed with multiple sclerosis. Since retiring he has established the Danny Wallace Foundation to provide aid for those suffering with the disease and completed the London Marathon in 2006 in five-and-a-half days in order to raise awareness.

Tommy Taylor, one of the eight 'Busby Babes' that died in the Munich air disaster, was born today in 1932. Taylor played for England in the 1954 World Cup and was one of the greatest centre forwards of his era, scoring 16 goals in 19 international appearances before his life was tragically cut short in 1958.

JANUARY 30

Despite his genius with the ball at his feet, Glenn Hoddle has never really had the people skills to match. Today in 1999 his infamous interview in the *Times* was published, where he gave his tuppence worth on reincarnation. 'You and I have been physically given two hands and two legs and half-decent brains,' he told Matt Dickinson. 'Some people have not been born like that for a reason. The karma is working from another lifetime…what you sow, you have to reap.' Controversy would ensue…

More woe for England today in 2006, as Multiplex, the company tasked with building the new Wembley Stadium, showed that their finishing was even worse than Andy Cole's, as they missed another deadline to hand the keys over.

JANUARY 31

Bobby Moore's first wife Tina put her ex-husband's collection of medals and trophies up for sale today in 1998, as she looked to secure the financial future for herself and her children. For a mere £2m you could have had your hands on Bobby's World Cup winner's medal, his solid gold Player of Players trophy from the tournament, his set of international caps from his 108 England appearances and his BBC Sports Personality of the Year gong.

Fabio Capello announced his first England squad today in 2008 and there was no room for his former Real Madrid charge David Beckham, due to a lack of match practice for the new LA Galaxy midfielder. There were no other real surprises in Capello's 30-man squad ahead of the friendly with Switzerland as he promised to take a further look at Beckham once he was up and running in the MLS.

ENGLAND
ON THIS DAY

FEBRUARY

February 1

'Anyone can be Luther Blissett simply by adopting the name Luther Blissett.' So reads the motto of the mysterious Luther Blissett project, a bizarre and loose collection of Italian subcultural activists who were behind a series of media hoaxes in the nineties. Their stunts included duping the media with a suspect story about a chimpanzee who was an award-winning artist, and the completely fictional disappearance of a conceptual artist who was tracing the word 'ART' across Europe. The group is, for no discernible reason, named after the former Watford, AC Milan and England striker who was born today in 1958.

Blissett became something of a joke after his disastrous spell in Italy where he scored just five goals in a whole season. Quite the contrast to Sir Stanley Matthews, football's first knight who was also born on this day in 1915.

February 2

Michael Owen's rise as a player in the Liverpool youth and then senior teams meant it was really a matter of if rather than when he would get his first call up to the England squad. It happened today in 1998 when Glenn Hoddle brought him into the senior England camp for the first time, for a friendly with Chile. He was only just 18 years old but would be a permanent fixture in the England squad until Fabio Capello became England coach in 2008.

A year later to the day and the manager who had given Owen his chance was out on his ear. Glenn Hoddle had some strange ideas (Eileen Drewery anyone?) and today he paid the price for airing his controversial views on karma in the *Times* three days earlier. After being slated by everyone from disabled rights campaigners to Prime Minister Tony Blair, karma caught up with Hoddle as he reaped what he had sown and was sacked today in 1999.

FEBRUARY 3

England lined up at Villa Park today in 1945 to play Scotland in a wartime international match. As well as well-known names like Stanley Matthews and Neil Franklin, there was also a man named Frank Wong Soo in the starting line up. Frank was the first ever non-white player to turn out for England and the only man of Chinese extraction ever to don the Three Lions. An inside-forward for Stoke City, Frank was born to a Chinese father and English mother in Buxton, Derbyshire. England beat Scotland 3-2 but sadly for Frank, the FA does not recognise his caps, as they were gained in unofficial friendly matches during World War Two.

Southampton and Tottenham striker Martin Chivers pulled on an England shirt for the first time today in 1971 when he made his debut in a European Championship qualifier against Malta in Gzira. Martin Peters got England's only goal in the 1-0 win, while Chivers went on to play 24 times for his country, scoring 13 goals.

FEBRUARY 4

England took on Wales today in 1888 in the Home Championship. Although the game was played at Nantwich Road, Crewe, it had been moved from the Racecourse Ground in Wrexham at the last minute and was officially classed as a Wales home game. England won 5-1 thanks to goals from George Woodhall, Tinsley Lindley and a Fred Dewhurst hat-trick. Woodhall's goal was the 100th scored by England who went on to win the championship while Wales had to settle for third.

Former England captain Alan Shearer broke Newcastle United's all-time scoring record today in 2006 when his 201st goal helped beat Portsmouth 2-0 at St James' Park. He took the record from Jackie Milburn, his predecessor in both the Newcastle and England attack.

FEBRUARY 5

English football – and football in general – has much to thank Charles Alcock for. The old Harrovian was a key figure in the development of the organised game and even invented the FA Cup, before captaining his own team Wanderers FC to victory in the inaugural competition. He can also be credited with inventing international football when a letter he wrote to *The Sportsman* newspaper was published on this day in 1870. In the letter he called for an England team to take on Scotland in a friendly match. Within two months the first unofficial international match took place in London. By November the first official game was played – a 0-0 draw – and international football was born.

Seven years later and England were getting rather good at it. Today in 1887 England's finest hit Ireland for seven without reply at Bramall Lane in the Home Championship.

FEBRUARY 6

One of the most tragic events in the history of English football occurred on this day in 1958. The Manchester United team were returning to England after a European Cup tie against Red Star Belgrade when their plane crashed on take-off in Munich. Twenty-three of the 44 people on board died in the crash or from injuries sustained in it, including a number of England players. Duncan Edwards, Roger Byrne, David Pegg and Tommy Taylor had all played for England before they died. Former Manchester City and England goalkeeper Frank Swift, who was on the trip as a journalist, also died in the crash.

The Wembley crowd observed a minute's silence for the Munich victims today in 2008 when England took on Switzerland in Fabio Capello's first game in charge. Typically of Capello's teams, England were not at their best but won all the same, goals from Jermaine Jenas and Shaun Wright-Phillips giving Capello a 2-1 win over the Swiss.

FEBRUARY 7

The pressure was beginning to build on Steve McClaren today in 2007 when his England team served up a lamentable display in a friendly against Spain at Old Trafford. Andrés Iniesta scored the only goal of the game but 'keeper Iker Casillas hardly had a save to make all night. The result meant England had failed to win in four matches but McClaren blamed absent players. He said: 'We were missing half a squad. We were without the likes of Owen Hargreaves, Wayne Rooney and John Terry – they're big players that can win you big games.' The fans weren't buying his excuses and booed the team off the pitch. Little did they know things would get far worse at the end of the year when England failed to qualify for Euro 2008.

Troubled midfielder Joey Barton made his England debut in the game, coming on for Frank Lampard 11 minutes before the final whistle. It was his one and only appearance for his country.

FEBRUARY 8

Another unhappy England reign was over today in 2012 when Fabio Capello resigned as England boss. Having failed to win over the players and overseen a limp tournament performance at the 2010 World Cup, Capello walked just four months before Euro 2012, with Roy Hodgson stepping in as his replacement.

After Don Revie quit as England boss suddenly in 1977 to coach the United Arab Emirates, the FA turned to the manager who had had a big hand in the 1966 World Cup win. Not Sir Alf Ramsey, but Ron Greenwood, the West Ham manager who had coached three key members of the England team at club level – Bobby Moore, Martin Peters and Geoff Hurst. Greenwood took England to the 1982 World Cup in Spain but went out at the group stage despite not losing a match. He resigned after England's exit and passed away on this day in 2006 aged 84.

FEBRUARY 9

These days top footballers earn millions through their basic salary, but before the Sky TV money came in players had to take every sponsorship opportunity that came their way. Today in 1977 Stan Bowles pulled off a cheeky move to maximise his pay-packet. The maverick forward was in the team to play Holland at Wembley and had been offered £200 by Gola to play in their boots, and £300 by Adidas to play in theirs. Legend has it Bowles wore one of each in the 2-0 defeat to Johan Cruyff's Holland side. England's first £1m player Trevor Francis made his England debut in the same game.

For almost as long as anyone can remember, England have struggled to find anyone to fill the problem position of left midfield. Middlesbrough's Stewart Downing became the latest player to give it a go today in 2005 when he made his England debut in a friendly against Holland at Villa Park. He came on for Shaun Wright-Phillips but couldn't make the difference in a 0-0 draw.

FEBRUARY 10

The England B team had an unbeaten record on home soil until today in 1998 when Chile won 2-1 at the Hawthorns. England dominated most of the match with Paul Merson pulling the strings in midfield but Manuel Neira struck twice in 12 minutes in the second half. Emile Heskey did pull one back late on but it was not enough to avoid defeat.

After Glenn Hoddle was sacked for his controversial comments on disabled people the FA turned to Howard Wilkinson to take charge of England for a friendly against France at Wembley on this day in 1999. Sergeant Wilko selected Lee Dixon for his first cap in five years but the England team was no match for World Champions France who won 2-0. Nicolas Anelka scored both goals for the French and very nearly became the first foreign player to score a hat-trick against England in England when he hit the bar late on.

FEBRUARY 11

In the days when he was still described as a wonderkid, Michael Owen made his England debut on this day in 1998. The young striker was selected by Glenn Hoddle for the first XI to play Chile in a friendly at Wembley. Owen failed to score against the South Americans who came away with a 2-0 win against an England line-up that included David Batty, Rob Lee and Dion Dublin. Marcelo Salas scored both goals for Chile.

Owen's long-time England teammate David Beckham was making headlines yet again today in 2009 when he equalled Bobby Moore's record of 108 caps for an outfield England player. Becks came on as a substitute in the 2-0 defeat for England to Spain in Seville. 'No-one can be compared to Bobby Moore because he's such a legend,' Becks said. 'He's a player I'll always look up to. I'm just very honoured to be even mentioned in the same breath as him.'

FEBRUARY 12

Legendary Everton striker Dixie Dean pulled on an England jersey for the first time on this day in 1927 to take on Wales in a Home International match at the Racecourse Ground in Wrexham. Predictably for a man who scored an incredible 383 goals in 433 appearances for Everton, Dean scored twice to help England to a 3-3 draw against the Welsh. His scoring record for England is just as impressive as it is for his club: in just 16 games for the Three Lions he scored 18 goals.

Another one-time Everton striker also made his England debut on this day. Wayne Rooney's first international appearance came in a farcical friendly against Australia at Upton Park in which Sven-Göran Eriksson substituted the entire starting XI at half-time. The senior team that played the first half were 2-0 down to the Socceroos before Francis Jeffers scored his only England goal in the second half. Brett Emerton added another late on to ensure England lost 3-1.

FEBRUARY 13

For a time during his reign as England manager Sven-Göran Eriksson was accused of being a little too liberal with the number of players upon whom he was choosing to bestow the honour of representing England or 'dishing out caps like sweets at a pantomime' as Brian Viner of the *Independent* put it. Three more newbies made their international debuts today in 2002 in a friendly against Holland in Amsterdam in preparation for the World Cup.

Southampton left-back Wayne Bridge looked comfortable in the England defence, but Aston Villa striker Darius Vassell grabbed the headlines with a classy goal and the man of the match award in the 1-1 draw. The other debutant was one-cap wonder Michael Ricketts who earned his spot after a red hot scoring streak for Bolton but soon after he faded away and ended his career with Tranmere Rovers.

FEBRUARY 14

Bobby Moore reached a personal landmark on this day in 1973 when he won his 100th England cap in a friendly match against Scotland at Hampden Park. Goals from Mick Channon, Martin Chivers, a brace from Allan Clarke and an own goal from Peter Lorimer gave England a 5-0 win – equalling Scotland's record home defeat in manager Willie Ormond's first game in charge.

England have faced Ireland twice on this day in history; the first was a comprehensive 4-0 win for the home side at Wolverhampton Wanderers' ground Molineux, but the Irish had their revenge today in 1914 when they comfortably beat England 3-0 at Ayresome Park in Middlesbrough with two goals from Billy Lacey and one from Billy Gillespie. It is Ireland's only three-goal win over England in 96 matches.

FEBRUARY 15

Hooliganism – termed 'the English disease' by the press – was back today in 1995 when England took on Ireland in a friendly match at Lansdowne Road. Jack Charlton's side went 1-0 up on 22 minutes when David Kelly scored and this triggered rioting among a group of English supporters. The premeditated violence escalated and as the Irish police struggled to restore order the referee led the players off the pitch and the match was abandoned – only the second England match in history that was not completed. No one was killed in the violence but many were injured and the sad inquest began into how it had happened.

The England v Ireland match was played out in its entirety today in 1913 at Windsor Park in Belfast and it was a landmark result for the hosts – their 2-1 win was the first time they had beaten England in 32 attempts. Billy Gillespie bagged both goals for Ireland, with Charlie Buchan scoring for England. Before this match England had won 28 and drawn three of their encounters with Ireland, scoring 150 goals in total and conceding just 19.

FEBRUARY 16

Managers today would kill for the longevity of Sir Walter Winterbottom. England's first ever full-time manager held the post for a staggering 16 years. A former Manchester United player, he did not have control over picking the England team which was done by committee, but he did lead the team through four World Cup campaigns. He was knighted in 1978 and passed away on this day in 2002, aged 89.

When England played Ireland today in 1907 at Goodison Park there was no manager, a board of selectors simply picked the team. England won 1-0 thanks to the only international goal of Harold Hardman's career.

FEBRUARY 17

Les Ferdinand made his England debut on this day in 1993. The former Newcastle, Tottenham and QPR striker was in Graham Taylor's starting line-up for the match against San Marino at Wembley and scored in the 6-0 win.

David Platt scored four goals in the match which equalled the record for an England player in a World Cup qualification match but he missed the chance to equal the overall record of five when San Marino goalkeeper Pierluigi Benedettini saved a last minute penalty from the former Juventus midfielder. Had he netted Platt would have joined Howard Vaughton, Steve Bloomer, Willie Hall and Malcolm Macdonald in the exclusive club of players to score five goals in the same match for England.

FEBRUARY 18

It was a baptism of fire for Ireland today in 1882 when they played their first ever international match, and got spanked a whopping 13-0 by England in Belfast. Howard Vaughton scored five, and his Aston Villa teammate Arthur Brown bagged four. It was the first time two players had got hat-tricks in an England match. The splendidly-named Horace Hutton Barnet did not score. It seems Ireland learned from their mistakes as this result remains their heaviest ever defeat.

England recorded another impressive away win today in 1987 when Gary Lineker scored four times to secure a 4-2 win against Spain in the Santiago Bernabéu in Madrid. Manager Bobby Robson gave Arsenal defender Tony Adams his debut in the game – he became the first player born after the 1966 World Cup final to play for England.

FEBRUARY 19

Today in 1870 was supposed to be the day the first ever England football team took to the pitch, but it wasn't. After early football pioneer Charles Alcock had advertised in *The Sportsman* newspaper for players to take part in the match that was to be England versus London-based Scots, but severe frost at The Oval caused the match to be postponed. It was played on March 5 but the 1-1 draw is not officially recognised as an England game.

Alan Shearer made his England debut on this day in 1992 when Graham Taylor selected him to start up front with Nigel Clough for a friendly against France at Wembley. Shearer started as he meant to go on and scored just before half-time to give England a 1-0 lead over a French side featuring Eric Cantona, then still playing for Leeds. In the second half Gary Lineker came on and proved he wasn't past it yet by adding another. It was his penultimate England goal.

FEBRUARY 20

England beat Ireland 6-0 today in 1897 at Trent Bridge with a hat-trick from Fred Wheldon, a brace from Steve Bloomer and one from Charlie Athersmith. Wheldon was one of England's best players and was also famous as a cricketer, playing for Worcestershire.

Paul Gascoigne hit a new low today in 2008 when he was arrested after he caused a disturbance at Gateshead's Hilton hotel. Its spokesman, Nigel Massey, told the *Guardian*: 'He had been an absolutely perfect guest; the staff loved him. On Wednesday morning the fire alarm went off at about 3am. Guests were aroused and the night porter came up and there was a bit of a confrontation. There was a bit of grabbing and a bit of verbal, but I'm told the porter is fine.' The former Spurs, Lazio and Rangers star was later sectioned under the Mental Health Act amid concerns about his increasingly erratic behaviour.

FEBRUARY 21

Duncan Edwards won 18 caps for England but would surely have gone on to win more than 100 had his life not tragically been cut short in the Munich air crash. Edwards did not die in the crash itself but suffered multiple leg breaks, fractured ribs and severely damaged kidneys. As he clung to life in hospital he kept a sense of humour, asking assistant manager Jimmy Murphy: 'What time is the kickoff against Wolves, Jimmy? I mustn't miss that match'. In the end his kidneys failed and he died on this day in 1958, aged just 21. English football had lost one of its future greats; in the words of his friend and teammate Bobby Charlton his death was 'the biggest single tragedy ever to happen to Manchester United and English football'.

The idea of an England B team was introduced by England's first manager Sir Walter Winterbottom as a way to introduce players to the international set up (the under-21 team was not established until 1976). England played their first ever B team match today in 1947 – a 0-0 draw against Switzerland's B team in Geneva.

FEBRUARY 22

Another day, another defeat to the Germans for England's finest. This time it wasn't in anything as important as a semi-final of a major competition so not too many tears were shed, and anyway it was a good few years before Gazza got near the England team. Today in 1978 Ron Greenwood joined the long list of England managers to have lost a match to the Germans when his side were beaten 2-1 in Munich. Stuart Pearson scored for England while Germany's goals came from Rainer Bonhof and Ronnie Worm.

For Kevin Keegan it was something of a local game. The permed one was playing for Hamburg at the time, although he was serving a Bundesliga suspension at the time of the game.

THE GREATEST MANAGER ENGLAND EVER HAD, SIR ALF RAMSEY, MEETS BRIAN CLOUGH, THE GREATEST THEY NEVER HAD

FEBRUARY 23

Football was mourning the loss of one of England's all-time great players today in 2000 when Sir Stanley Matthews died aged 85. Sir Stan was the first footballer to be knighted and the first ever recipient of the Ballon d'Or. He was a national hero who played in the First Division when he was 50 years old. Sir Bobby Robson said: 'He had immense skill – great skill off the ball, a beautiful dribbler. He was one of the greatest players the game has ever seen. He ranks alongside players like Pele, Maradona and Cruyff – and he was one of ours.' Pele himself said of Matthews: 'The man who taught us the way football should be played.'

Exactly 111 years before, Stoke City's Victoria Ground where Sir Stan strutted his stuff for so long, hosted an England international against Wales. An estimated 6,000 strong crowd saw England win 4-1.

FEBRUARY 24

After dishing out a 13-0 hammering to Ireland in the first match between the two, England took on the Irish again today in 1883, this time at Liverpool Cricket Ground at Aigburth Park. It was the first time Ireland played in England but it was not a happy experience – they lost 7-0, reducing their captain to tears.

Bobby Moore is the only English captain to lift the World Cup, and he sadly died on this day in 1993. Moore was manager Alf Ramsey's lieutenant on the field and it was his defensive surety and leadership that drove England to World Cup glory in 1966. In 1993 he announced he was suffering from cancer. His last public appearance was at England's match against San Marino on February 17th which he commentated on for radio. He died within a week. Years earlier Alf Ramsey had said of him: 'My captain, my leader, my right-hand man. He was the spirit and the heartbeat of the team. He was the supreme professional, the best I ever worked with. Without him England would never have won the World Cup.'

FEBRUARY 25

England beat Ireland 6-1 today in 1893 in a friendly match played in Birmingham but the most notable performance was from Walter Gilliat. An Oxford graduate, Gilliat scored a hat-trick on his debut for England, but even this was not enough to cement a place in the side and it remained his one and only England appearance. Albert Allen and Jack Yates also achieved this unlikely feat, also both against Ireland in 1888 and 1889 respectively.

England beat Belgium 3-1 today in 1970 in a friendly in Brussels with a goal from Geoff Hurst and a brace for Alan Ball. Skipper Bobby Moore was making his 75th appearance for England while Peter Osgood won the first of just four caps he would notch up in his career.

FEBRUARY 26

Wayne Rooney was not the first 17-year-old to play for England; he was beaten to that record by Tot Rostron who was 17 years and 311 days old when he made his England debut on this day in 1881. Rostron couldn't prevent England losing 1-0 to Wales in the friendly match.

Alan Shearer shocked England fans today in 2000 when he announced he was to quit the international team after Euro 2000. The England captain said: 'I want everyone to understand that I am not walking away from a challenge – I am hugely patriotic and my time as England captain has made me incredibly proud. However, I realise that if I want to give Newcastle value for money in the remaining four years of my contract with them, I will need to pace myself a bit more than I am able to do at the moment.' Manager Kevin Keegan said: 'Of course I was very sad, and I tried to persuade him to change his mind, but everyone should respect his decision.'

FEBRUARY 27

Alf Ramsey, the only England coach to have delivered the World Cup, took charge of his first match with the national team on this day in 1962. The former Ipswich Town boss took over from Walter Winterbottom in the England hot-seat but his reign did not get off to a very promising start. In a European preliminary match away to France, Alf's England team featuring Bobby Moore, Jimmy Greaves and Bobby Charlton was humbled 5-2. Bobby Tambling and Robert Smith scored for England.

Joe Mercer was the man who took charge of England following Sir Alf's sacking, but today in 1943 Joe was playing for the national team in a wartime international against Wales at Wembley which England won 5-3.

FEBRUARY 28

On this day in 2001, England's first foreign manager, Sven-Göran Eriksson, was in the dug-out for the first time overseeing his new team. It was a great start for the Swede as his side beat Spain at Villa Park 3-0. Perhaps already gaining an appreciation of a slight tendency among the English media and fans to get carried away, Sven was urging caution after the match. 'You win a friendly, even if it's against Spain 3-0, but you must try to keep your feet on the floor,' he said, anticipating the inevitable failure of the team at the World Cup the following year. 'Don't try to fly and say you've won the World Cup. That would be a big mistake,' he added.

These days of course to reach the World Cup finals you have to go through a testing qualification process. Not so for the first World Cup in 1930 when all you had to do was reply to an invitation to take part. The deadline for entries for the competition in Uruguay was on this day in 1930. Brazil, Argentina, Peru, Paraguay, Bolivia, Chile, the USA and Mexico all replied, England didn't bother.

FEBRUARY 29

Trevor Francis is famous as the first £1m player in British football, but less well known is Alf Common who was the first £1,000 footballer. Sunderland sold the striker to Middlesbrough for the landmark fee in 1905. He scored on his debut and helped the team avoid relegation. On this day in 1904 Alf made his England debut against Wales at the Racecourse Ground in Wrexham. He didn't score that day but did grab two goals on his second England appearance two weeks later against Ireland.

Alf would have been proud of his former club today in 2004 when Middlesbrough broke their 128-year trophy drought and won the League Cup. Steve McClaren's side beat Sam Allardyce's Bolton Wanderers 2-1 in the final in Cardiff thanks to an early goal from Joseph-Désiré Job and a penalty from Boudewijn Zenden. Kevin Davies pulled one back for Bolton but it was not enough and Boro had won a major trophy for the first time in their history. The two managers would again face off against each other in the race to succeed Sven-Göran Eriksson as England boss in 2006.

ENGLAND
ON THIS DAY

MARCH

MARCH 1

Joe Cole's injury-time winner gave the Anfield crowd something to cheer when England beat Uruguay 2-1 today in 2006. Following Omar Pouso's stunning 30-yard volley, Peter Crouch came on as a second-half substitute to equalise with his first goal for the national team. This was after a blunder by the kitman saw the leggy striker come on with the number 21 on his chest and shorts, but a 12 on his back. A minute's silence was held and black armbands worn in honour of former Chelsea striker Peter Osgood who had died earlier that day and Ron Greenwood who had passed away the month before.

In 1980 England fans were mourning another great, as Dixie Dean, one of English football's greatest ever goalscorers died aged 73 whilst watching his beloved Everton take on Liverpool in the Merseyside derby at Goodison Park. Despite only turning out 16 times for England Dean hit the back of the net 18 times.

MARCH 2

After giving David Beckham and England fans nine months to stew on Becks' red card in the France 98 second-round clash, today in 1999 Diego Simeone 'fessed up and admitted that he had conned the referee into red carding the midfielder. 'Let's just say the referee fell into the trap. You could say that my falling transformed a yellow card into a red card,' he sneered. 'Obviously, I was being clever. By letting myself fall, I got the referee to pull out a red card immediately.'

It was another bad day for England in 1878 when they took on Scotland at the original Hampden Park stadium, as the Scots put seven past England in a 7-2 victory. Along with Hungary's 1954 assault on the England goal, this remains the only time England have conceded so many. A match report in *Bell's Life*, by 'A Disgusted Englishman' read: 'The England players we had down this time were a splendid lot of players individually, but to my idea they played very selfishly, each one of them appearing to play for himself and not the success of the side.' Sounds awfully familiar...

MARCH 3

England suffered a 3-1 defeat to Scotland on this day in 1877 at a wet Kennington Oval. William Lindsay was playing for the Three Lions, despite turning out for the Scots in the 1870 unofficial internationals and having been born in India. Alfred Lyttelton scored for England but a brace for John Ferguson either side of a James Richmond strike was enough to seal victory for the visitors – who had four players named John in the team.

Today in 1894 England were racking up their 50th game when they took on Ireland at the charmingly named venue of Solitude. A late Irish equaliser from William Gibson saw the sides draw 2-2, despite England playing with ten men for 70 minutes after captain Bob Holmes went down injured.

MARCH 4

England and Scotland met for the fifth time today in 1876 in a match that saw the first ever half-time break. Until then teams had merely changed ends and got on with the game after 45 minutes, but the 15,000 fans in attendance at Hamilton Crescent in Partick were given the chance to nip to the loo at the break, with the home side 3-0 up. The Scots would hold on to this lead as they recorded their second win over England in a game that also saw the introduction of the crossbar, replacing tape between the posts.

In somewhat of a pointless exercise, Pele today in 2004 revealed the list of his top 100 living footballers as part of the 100th anniversary of Fifa. Ever the diplomat, Pele had not wanted to upset anyone, as several players seemed to be included on political grounds, but the Brazilian found room for seven England players: Gordon Banks, David Beckham, Bobby Charlton, Kevin Keegan, Gary Lineker, Michael Owen and Alan Shearer.

MARCH 5

Although the record book marks the 1872 match between England and Scotland as the first official international match, the two foes met today in 1870 in the first of two unofficial clashes. It was Charles Alcock, the man who invented the FA Cup, that initiated the game, throwing down the gauntlet to the Scots when he placed adverts in a number of Scottish newspapers. A frightfully upper-class affair, the Scots could boast then-Prime Minister William Gladstone's son in defence. The teams drew 1-1 thanks to a late long-range equaliser from Scotland's Mr R.E. Crawford when England decided to throw caution to the wind and remove their goalie in what *The Sporting Gazette* described as a match 'that was throughout distinguished by skill, determination and "dash" on the part of both teams.'

Today in 1892 England notched up their 150th goal, when they downed Wales 2-0 at the Racecourse Ground in Wrexham. Arthur Henfrey of Corinthians' opener in the 15th minute was the landmark goal, coming after only 44 matches. England were captained that day by the delightfully-named Harry Daft.

MARCH 6

Today in 1875 England and Scotland duelled for the fourth time when they met at the Kennington Oval in London. England had to start with only ten men as goalkeeper William Carr arrived 15 minutes late. Forward Alexander Bonsor took his place in goal, letting Henry McNiel put the Scots ahead just before Carr arrived. Charles Alcock, the driving force behind the new international scene, was captain in his only ever official international and scored to put his side ahead in the 65th minute, but Peter Andrews would peg the Three Lions back with a 70th minute strike.

Derek Kevan, the West Brom centre forward nicknamed 'The Tank', who scored twice for England in the 1958 World Cup was born today in 1935.

MARCH 7

More England v Scotland action today in 1874, as England would suffer their first ever loss. This was the two teams' third encounter and was played out at the West of Scotland Cricket Ground in Partick in front of 7,000 fans. England took an early lead through Robert Kingsford, scoring in his only ever game, but goals either side of the half-time change-around saw Scotland clock up their first ever win. In possibly the first-ever case of fixture pile-ups Wanderers FC duo Hubert Heron and John Hawley Edwards had played three days earlier when their club side defeated Westminster School 4-0.

The 'forgotten five' of England's finest hour were finally honoured by the Queen today in 2000, when World Cup winners Nobby Stiles, Alan Ball, Roger Hunt, Ray Wilson and George Cohen became the last of the '66 squad to receive MBEs at Buckingham Palace.

MARCH 8

He'd won the World Cup, been given an OBE and made arguably the greatest save of all time, but surely none of this could prepare him for being presented with the 'big red book' when he appeared on *This Is Your Life* today in 1972. Gordon Banks was enjoying some of the finest form of his career at this point, finishing the season as the Football Writers' Association Footballer of the Year, but his career would come to an abrupt end later that year when he lost an eye in a car crash.

England's first win came today in 1873 when they beat Scotland 4-2 in their second ever game. A frantic match saw both sides adopt a 2-2-6 formation as an excitable crowd of around 3,000 repeatedly spilled onto the pitch, holding the game up on several occasions. Scotland could only afford eight train tickets to London, so were forced into picking three London-based residents for the game at the Oval. William Kenyon-Slaney, who was also MP for Newport Salop, was England's hero of the day, bagging the team's first ever goal on his one and only international appearance.

MARCH 9

The Terry Venables era got underway today in 1994 when he took charge of his first game, a friendly with Denmark at Wembley as England looked to rebound from their failure to reach the 1994 World Cup. El Tel used the game to hand debuts to three players, Graeme le Saux, Darren Anderton and Matt le Tissier. A solitary goal from skipper David Platt gave England a 1-0 win over the reigning European champions.

More goals were on show today in 1895, when England took Ireland to the sword, crushing them 9-0 in Derby. Steve Bloomer staked a claim as football's first superstar, scoring twice on his debut as he would go on net 28 times in his 23 England appearances. The Derby and Middlesbrough inside-right was also credited with having the first celebrity 'WAG' when he married Sarah Walker in 1896. After he hung up his boots Bloomer moved to coach Britannia Berlin in 1914, but unlike on the football pitch, his timing was off and he was interned in a civilian detention camp when World War One broke out. After the war he moved to Spain where he would lead Real Union to a Copa del Rey victory in 1924.

MARCH 10

England lost out again to Scotland on this day in 1883, with the visitors taking a 3-2 win at a snowy Bramall Lane in Sheffield, in what was their 18th meeting.

Less than six months after leaving his cushy job as the FA technical director to take over struggling Sunderland, Howard Wilkinson was sacked today in 2003. The former England caretaker manager, and last Englishman to win the league title during his time at Leeds United, had obviously lost his touch in the dug-out, winning only two out of 20 league games as the Black Cats limped towards a then-record low total of 19 points in the Premiership that season.

MARCH 11

A new rule was introduced when England took on Scotland today in 1882, giving the referee the power to award a goal if a deliberate handball had prevented the ball hitting the back of the net. It didn't do England much good however, as they went down 5-1 at Hampden Park. Turning out for Scotland was Andrew Watson who was the first-ever mixed-race international footballer. The curiously-named Doctor Greenwood was making his final appearance for England.

In 1912 England bagged their fifth win in a row against Wales when they defeated the Dragons 2-0 at the Racecourse Ground in Wrexham. The goalscorers that day were Sunderland's George Holley and Burnley's Bert Freeman as England set up a Home Championship decider with Scotland later that month that ended in a 1-1 draw, giving both sides a share of the title.

MARCH 12

Pint-size 1966 hero Alan Ball put on the captain's armband for the first time today in 1975 when England took on West Germany in a friendly at Wembley. The midfielder inspired his side to a 2-0 win over the Germans with debutant Malcolm Macdonald opening his scoring account in the process. Ball would retain the armband for the remaining five games of his England career, before bowing out against Scotland at the end of the 1974/75 season.

Another first cap goal-getter was John Veitch who managed three in England's 5-1 win over Wales today in 1894. Despite his antics in front of goal he would never play for England again and joins Albert Allen, Frank Bradshaw, Walter Gilliat and John Yates as the only players to have scored a hat-trick on their one and only England appearance.

MARCH 13

Caps were dished out for the first time today in 1886 for the XI that took on Ireland at Ballynafeigh Park in Belfast. The idea was proposed by N. Lane Jackson, founder of the Corinthians who came up with the idea to give out a white silk cap with a red rose embroidered on the front. Benjamin Spilsbury certainly earned his new headwear, scoring four times as England cruised to a 6-1 win in the Home Championship match.

There was a Glasgow goal-fest in 1880, when Scotland defeated their oldest rivals 5-4. England have never scored so many goals and ended up on the losing side and fielded the unfortunately named Segal Bastard in what was probably not the only use of bad language that day.

MARCH 14

Today in 1874 Alfred George Goodwyn was unfortunate enough to be the first-ever international footballer to die. Goodwyn had represented England as a defender in the 1873 match against Scotland, where the *Glasgow Herald* described his play as 'faultless', but as part of the Royal Engineers was summoned back to India where he would die of injuries suffered in a riding accident. A bad day for the regiment was compounded when their football team lost the FA Cup final 2-0 to Oxford University back in England.

Charles Buchan, the Sunderland and Arsenal centre forward, captained England for the first time today in 1921 as they drew 0-0 with Wales in Wrexham. Buchan's England career was curtailed by the First World War, but after hanging up his boots he would go on to launch *Charles Buchan's Football Monthly*, the world's first ever specialist football magazine which ran for over twenty years.

MARCH 15

England sent out two teams to play today in 1890, as a professional XI hopped on the ferry to Ireland to complete a 9-1 win and an amateur side won 3-1 against Wales. Fred Geary of Everton made his debut against the Irish, scoring a hat-trick in the first of his two England appearances. Ireland's goalscorer in that game was John Reynolds, who would later turn out for England, making eight appearances for the Three Lions.

The first ever all-ticket match took place at Cathkin Park in Glasgow on this day in 1884 with the Scots making sure the 10,000 home fans in attendance went home happy, as John Smith would score the only goal of the game as the Scots made it five wins in a row against the Three Lions.

MARCH 16

Goals galore today, as England have a habit of beating up on the Welsh on this day. In 1896 it was the turn of Steve Bloomer to shine, as he scored five in England's 9-1 romp at Arms Park in Cardiff. His first was England's 200th goal and the five-goal haul of his remains the joint highest tally in a single game. Corinthians centre forward Gilbert Oswald Smith, who was considered by many to be the best player of the 19th century, added two goals to the scoresheet.

In 1908 England could only manage to win 7-1 against Wales, with prolific Spurs striker Vivian Woodward scoring a hat-trick. Wales 'keeper Leigh Roose didn't fancy soldiering on when he was injured in the first half, so was replaced at half-time by David Davies in what was the first occurrence of a substitution during an England game.

MARCH 17

England took on Wales in the Home Championship today in 1913, handing debuts to no less than eight players for the clash at Bristol's Ashton Gate. A rip-roaring first half saw the teams go in even at three goals each, but debutant Harry Hampton would strike in the second half to give England a 4-3 win to set up a winner takes all decider against Scotland, where Hampton would again strike, scoring the game's only goal to hand the title to England.

England played their first match of the twentieth century today in 1900, facing off against Ireland in Dublin. Harry Johnson and Charlie Sagar both scored on their debut to give England a winning start in their second century, although this would be their win only in the 1900 Home Championship.

MARCH 18

Five days after all football in the UK had been shut down as a result of the coronavirus pandemic, Uefa confirmed on this day in 2020 that Euro 2020 was postponed for a year. England had breezed through qualifying, with Harry Kane's 12 goals helping Gareth Southgate's men rack up seven wins in their eight Group A matches, but the biggest crisis to grip post-war football put the brakes on the pan-European tournament which was due to be played in 12 cities across 12 countries to mark the competition's 60th anniversary. The decision came shortly after England's friendlies against Denmark and Italy, due to be played at the end of March, were postponed.

Steve Bloomer was in typical rampant form against Wales today in 1901 at St James' Park in Newcastle. The Derby hot-shot grabbed four of England's goals in a 6-0 triumph, reaffirming his place as England's first-ever superstar and putting his country well on the way to that season's Home Championship title.

MARCH 19

There was another England v Wales clash today in 1906, with the two sides meeting at Arms Park. A late goal from Samuel Day gave England a narrow 1-0 victory meaning Wales' win drought against the English continued as they looked for their first success in this fixture since 1882. Robert Evans, who played outside-left for Wales was of the attitude of 'if you can't beat them, join them', as five years later he defected to England, winning four caps to add to his ten appearances for Wales after the FA decreed that the Chester-born Evans should not be eligible for Wales despite having Welsh parents.

England's 3-2 loss to Scotland today in 1887 had far-reaching consequences, as it would be the last match where the team were selected by the FA Council. England toiled in the snow at Leamington Road in Blackburn and having not beaten the old enemy for eight years, the powers that be decided that changes were needed. A new seven-man FA International Select Committee was then formed to pick England's team for their next game, against Wales the following year.

MARCH 20

Showing some textbook FA incompetence on a par with appointing Steve McClaren, the Jules Rimet trophy was stolen today in 1966 whilst under the watch of England's powers-that-be. The trophy was on display at Central Hall in Westminster when thieves outwitted two security guards, causing the FA to secretly create a replica whilst the police struggled to make any inroads into the case. Eventually, where the Metropolitan Police Force failed, a small dog named Pickles succeeded, tracking down the famous trophy wrapped in newspaper under a south London hedge a week later.

Back in 1899 England were celebrating a 4-0 win over the Welsh, that man Steve Bloomer again leading the line with two goals for the Three Lions at Ashton Gate.

MARCH 21

Scotland dashed England's chances of winning their first-ever Home Nations title today in 1885, when they held them to a 1-1 draw at the Oval. Charlie Bambridge's equalising goal for the Three Lions did mean, however, that Scotland's record-breaking run of 12 successive wins was ended, but the Scots bounced back two days later to thrash Wales 8-1 and secure the second ever Home Championship title.

The man considered to be the best manager England never had – by himself at least – was born today in 1935. Brian Clough would have surely had a sizeable impact on the pitch for England had his playing career not been prematurely curtailed by a cruciate ligament injury suffered on Boxing Day 1962, when he was playing for Sunderland against Bury. During his time at Roker Park he scored 54 goals in 61 appearances, following on from an equally productive spell at Middlesbrough where he netted 197 times in 213 games. His two caps for England both came in 1959, but he failed to score against Wales and Sweden.

MARCH 22

England put eight goals past San Marino on this day in 2013 in a World Cup qualifier that BBC chief football writer Phil McNulty branded 'as close to being a pointless exercise as international football gets'. Alex Oxlade-Chamberlain, Jermain Defoe, Ashley Young, Frank Lampard, Wayne Rooney and Daniel Sturridge all scored as England coasted to their biggest win since an 8-0 battering of Turkey at Wembley in 1987.

By 1888 international football looked as though it was here to stay, as England's leading clubs met to sound out the creation of the Football League today at Anderton's Hotel in Fleet Street.

MARCH 23

In 1988 England offered their fans a sneak preview of what to expect in that summer's upcoming European Championships when they took on Holland in a friendly at Wembley. Despite taking an early lead through Gary Lineker, England, and particularly Tony Adams, suffered a calamitous spell that saw Holland take a 2-1 lead into the break, thanks to a Jonny Bosman strike and an Adams own goal. Things did get better for the Arsenal centre-back though as he scored a second-half equaliser as the match finished 2-2, but the less said about his performance against the Dutch later that year the better...

England's women fared better today in 2001 though, as they recorded an impressive 4-2 win over Spain in a friendly at Kenilworth Road – naturally this was before women's rights champion Mike Newell was made Luton manager. The game was preparation for that summer's upcoming European Championship, where England's early promise failed to materialise and they were dumped out in the group stage.

MARCH 24

Two years late and £400m over budget, the new Wembley Stadium finally hosted its first game today in 2007, with an under-21 match between England and Italy. Azzurri youngster Giampaolo Pazzini had the honour of scoring the first goal under the new arch, and would go on to score the first hat-trick in a 3-3 draw. David Bentley scored England's first goal at their new home.

Manager Don Revie took today's match against Wales at the Racecourse Ground in Wrexham as a chance to experiment, handing debuts to eight players in the Welsh FA Centenary International. Debut goals from Ray Kennedy and Peter Taylor gave Revie's boys a 2-1 win.

MARCH 25

Kenneth Wolstenholme, the man who uttered English football's most famous words died today in 2002. Wolstenholme flew over 100 RAF missions over Germany during World War II before becoming an integral part of the BBC's football coverage, covering every FA Cup Final between 1949 and 1971, as well as all manner of European and World Cup finals. However, he will forever be remembered for uttering the phrase: 'Some people are on the pitch… they think it's all over! … It is now!'

It was all over for Gary Mabbutt and Mark Hateley's England careers today in 1992 as they bowed out in England's friendly with Czechoslovakia in Prague. Scoring their first goals in England's 2-2 draw that day were the Arsenal duo of Paul Merson and Martin Keown.

MARCH 26

England's 2-0 win over Spain in the Camp Nou today in 1980 notched up its fair share of milestones. Coming on as a second-half substitute was Emlyn Hughes who became the only player to be capped in the 1960s, '70s and '80s. His former Liverpool teammate Kevin Keegan, now at Hamburg won his 50th cap, as the Three Lions won 2-0 thanks to goals from Tony Woodcock and Trevor Francis.

The accomplishments of Hughes and Keegan received only a fraction of the media attention that David Beckham basked in today in 2008 when he finally made his 100th England appearance in a friendly against France in Paris. Becks was the fifth player to reach a ton for the Three Lions, but Franck Ribéry spoilt his big day, scoring the only goal to give the home side a 1-0 win.

MARCH 27

Kevin Keegan exploded onto the international managerial scene today, taking charge of England for the first time and recording a 3-1 win over Poland in a Euro 2000 qualifier at Wembley. The secret to his success that day was telling Paul Scholes to 'go out and drop hand grenades.' The Manchester United midfielder willingly obliged, scoring a stunning hat-trick and Keegan's 18-month rollercoaster ride in the England hot-seat began.

England took on Jack Charlton's Republic of Ireland side in a European Championship qualifier today in 1991, with goals from former Arsenal teammates Lee Dixon and Niall Quinn ensuring that honours were even, in a match that saw Lee Sharpe make his England debut. The next time the two sides met – at Lansdowne Road in 1995 – the game was abandoned following crowd trouble.

MARCH 28

Steve McClaren was feeling the pressure today after his charges limped to an unimpressive 3-0 win over the assorted postmen and plumbers making up the Andorran national football team. 'Gentlemen,' he said to the media scrum following the game, 'if you want to write whatever you want to write, you can write it because that is all I'm going to say.' He then stormed out and the hacks had a field day.

The beleaguered former Middlesbrough boss could have done with the likes of Reginald Erskin 'Tip' Foster in his line up. The Corinthian inside-forward made his debut for England in their 1-1 draw with Wales today in 1900 and stands alone in sporting lexicon as the only man to captain England at both football and cricket. His debut Test knock of 287 remains the highest score by a player in his first Test and he also managed three goals in his five England appearances on the football field.

MARCH 29

One of England's most infamous one-cap wonders strutted his stuff today, when William 'Fatty' Foulke made his only international appearance against Wales in 1897. Standing 6ft 6in and tipping the scales at 24 stone, the Sheffield United 'keeper was believed to have been the first target of the 'who ate all the pies?' terrace chant and proved to be enough of an obstacle to keep out the Welsh, as England recorded a 4-0 win. Whilst at Chelsea a report at the time claimed Foulke apparently 'got into the dining-room before the rest of the team and polished off all 11 breakfasts. In response to the remonstrations of his teammates he only replied: "I don't care what you call me, so long as you don't call me late for lunch."'

Fast-forward to 2000 and Staffordshire University today announced they were giving students the chance to study David Beckham as a part of their degree. The football culture module put Goldenballs in the spotlight, focusing on his haircuts, marriage to Posh and his sending off in the 1998 World Cup. Who says education is wasted on the young?

MARCH 30

Despite the modern-day cliché of 'there's no easy games in international football', Luxembourg have never really posed a problem for England, with the Three Lions clocking up 47 goals to Luxembourg's three in the nine matches the pair have contested. Don Revie's men took on the minnows today in 1977, with England's first £1m-man Trevor Francis scoring his first goal for the national team in a 5-0 canter for England.

England's performance against another of international football's lesser lights, Azerbaijan, was less impressive today in 2005, when second-half goals from Steven Gerrard and David Beckham saved Sven's blushes at St James' Park in this 2006 World Cup qualifier.

MARCH 31

Arsenal's England midfielder David Rocastle tragically died today in 2001 aged 33 from non-Hodgkin's lymphoma. Prior to the 1990 World Cup it looked as though Rocky was set to become one of his generation's key players in the England team, but fate had other ideas and a mixture of injuries and lack of form meant his career petered out and came to a premature end after a loan spell at Hull City in 1998.

Scotland had endured a disappointing Home Championship challenge in the 1927/28 season, so when the auld enemy travelled down to Wembley today in 1928, little was expected of them. England had also flattered to deceive that season, meaning the match was a wooden spoon contest. It took only three minutes for Scotland to take the lead, when Alex Jackson scored the first of his three goals that afternoon, as they would romp to a 5-1 win, inflicting England's first loss at Wembley. A breathless report in *The Observer* described the ease with which Scotland tore though their oldest rivals: 'Once were counted 15 consecutive passes from Scot to Scot. England were as helpless as small boys chasing a butterfly.'

ENGLAND
ON THIS DAY

APRIL

APRIL 1

England took on Scotland today in 1893 in front of an estimated 15,000 strong crowd at the Richmond Athletic Ground in London. With just over 30 minutes left to play England were trailing 2-1, after the opener from RC Gosling was bettered by goals from Tommy Waddell and Bill Sellar. On 58 minutes the England fightback began when George Cotterill equalised. Fred Spiksley added two more before Jack Reynolds finished off the scoring to give England a 5-2 win.

Under Fabio Capello England won all eight of his first competitive matches in charge. Today in 2009 their 100 per cent record came closest to slipping when they faced the Ukraine at Wembley in a World Cup qualifier. After Peter Crouch had given England the lead, Andriy Shevchenko equalised for the away side with 15 minutes left. It fell to captain John Terry to score the winner just five minutes before full time.

APRIL 2

Jack Reynolds made his England debut on this day in 1892 against Scotland at Ibrox, but it was not his first taste of international football. In the previous two years Reynolds had played five times for Ireland before it emerged he was actually English. He even scored for Ireland against England in a game in March 1890. He did not score on his debut but did manage three goals in his England career against Wales and Scotland. He remains the only man in history to have scored for and against England.

England took on Scotland again on this day in 1955, this time at Wembley Stadium in the Home Championship. A 7-2 win for England was rounded off nicely by Dennis Wilshaw who scored four goals – he was the first man to score a hat-trick for England against Scotland (since matched only by Jimmy Greaves), and remains the only player to have bagged four against the Scots in an England shirt.

APRIL 3

After poor finishing and the heroics of goalkeeper Jan Tomaszewski meant England could only draw 1-1 with Poland and did not therefore qualify for the 1974 World Cup, the writing was on the wall for the manager Sir Alf Ramsey. Today in 1974 he took charge of England for the very last time. A limp 0-0 draw against Portugal in the Estadio da Luz in Lisbon was all his team could manage. He was sacked shortly afterwards.

Sunderland defender Dave Watson and Queens Park Rangers forward Stan Bowles both made their England debuts in this match. For Bowles, it was the first of just five caps he won in his career, but it was the first of 65 times Watson would don an England jersey, which is a record for an England player without ever playing at the World Cup finals – he was left out of Ron Greenwood's squad for Spain 1982.

APRIL 4

England were beaten 2-1 by Scotland today in 1896 in a match at Celtic Park. The win for Scotland ended England's run of 20 matches without defeat – still a record for the team. The last time England had lost was also against Scotland, two years before in the Home Championship when the Scots won at Leamington Road, Blackburn, by three goals to two.

It was also against Scotland, on this day in 1914, that Frederick Waldren made his England debut in a match at Crystal Palace. The Tottenham winger, known as Fanny, was just 5ft 2ins tall, making him the shortest player ever to play for England. He got just two caps, albeit eight years apart. His second England appearance came after World War One, against Wales in 1922.

APRIL 5

When Wayne Rooney made his England debut in 2003 aged 17 years and 111 days he broke a record that had stood for almost 124 years. Rooney displaced James Prinsep as the youngest ever England player, who played his only match in England colours today in 1879 against Scotland at the Oval.

Today in 1902 was one of those mercifully rare but tragic days when what started out as a football match ended up as a disaster claiming many lives. The England team travelled up to Glasgow to play Scotland at Ibrox but, at 51 minutes and the scores tied at 1-1, the newly-built West Tribune Stand collapsed because of heavy rainfall the previous night. Hundreds of fans fell up to 40 feet, 25 were killed and more than 500 injured.

APRIL 6

There were mixed fortunes for England players today in 1907 when they took on Scotland at St James' Park in Newcastle. Bob Crompton scored after just two minutes but sadly for him it was at the wrong end. Just before half-time Steve Bloomer scored England's equaliser – it was his 28th goal in just 23 England appearances. It was also the last time the Derby County legend played for his country.

Anglo-German relations were tested again on this day in 1994 when the FA decided to pull out of a proposed friendly match against Germany scheduled to be played on April 20 – Adolf Hitler's birthday. Both pro and anti Nazi groups were planning protests and the FA feared that the match would become 'a focus for disorder'. Otto Johne, head of the Berlin branch of Germany's football federation said: 'It's an outrage. We are extremely disappointed and depressed by this decision. It's bad for sport when a tiny minority of extremists succeed like this. They're making April 20 a day of glory for the Nazis again.'

APRIL 7

Albert Allen made his England debut on this day in 1888 in a Home Championship match against Ireland at the Ulster Cricket Ground in Belfast. He had an absolute stormer and bagged a hat-trick as England won 5-1. Even this was not enough to keep his place in the team and he never played for the national team again. He is one of a select band of five men, along with Walter Gilliat and Jack Yates, who have scored a hat-trick on their only England appearance.

Maverick England captain Stanley Harris played his last game for England on this day in 1906 at Hampden Park against Scotland. With England losing 2-0 Harris instructed his whole team to take up positions within 20 yards of the Scots' goal. England lost the match 2-1, Harris never played for England again, and within the year the International Board had altered the offside rule so no player could be offside in his own half to avoid any team repeating Harris's trick.

APRIL 8

England played Scotland today in 1899 with the Home Championship trophy up for grabs for the winning side. Going into the game both teams had four points after both had defeated Ireland and Wales. England proved too strong for the Scots, beating them 2-1 at Villa Park with goals from Gilbert Oswald Smith and Jimmy Settle.

Former England player Billy Bassett was one of football's earliest celebrities and played more than 260 games for West Bromwich Albion in a 13-year one-club career. He played 16 times for England, scoring eight goals and gained half his caps against the auld enemy Scotland. Such was his dislike for the Scots after facing them on the football field so many times, that in 29 years as chairman of West Brom he never once signed a Scotsman to play for the club. He died on this day in 1937 aged 68. More than 100,000 people lined the streets of West Bromwich for his funeral.

APRIL 9

Scotland beat England 1-0 at Wembley on this day in 1938, with Tommy Walker grabbing the only goal. Bill Shankly was in the Scotland team while Stan Cullis, Stanley Matthews and Cliff Bastin all played for England. The celebrated *Daily Express* football writer Henry Rose was not much impressed by the football on show. 'Most of the match, I was a Rose between two yawns,' he wrote drily in his report. Twenty years later, Rose was one of the eight sports journalists who died in the Munich air crash.

England also took on Scotland on this day in 1904, this time at Celtic Park. Again the score was 1-0 to the visiting team. Steve Bloomer scored the only goal of the game with a powerful shot. Scottish goalkeeper Peter McBride said: 'I had no more chance of catching that shot than a snowball in Hades.'

APRIL 10

Sheffield Wednesday's Hillsborough ground hosted a match between England and Scotland on this day in 1920. At half-time Scotland were sitting pretty at 4-2 up but in the second period two England debutants fired England ahead with three goals to win the game 5-4. Bob Kelly of Burnley scored twice and Fred Morris of West Brom added another to cap a dramatic win for England. It would be Morris's only England goal of his career while Kelly scored a further seven in 14 appearances for his country.

Two World Cup winners made their England debuts today in 1965 when the Three Lions took on Scotland at Wembley in the Home Championship and Jack Charlton and Nobby Stiles got their first taste of international football. Jackie's brother Bobby bagged one of England's goals in a 2-2 draw but more importantly manager Sir Alf Ramsey had found two more pieces of the jigsaw that would help him win the World Cup the following year.

APRIL 11

A bittersweet day for England today in 1964 when they lost 1-0 to Scotland at Hampden Park in the Home Championship. Alan Gilzean scored for Scotland to give them the win but it wasn't enough to prevent England winning the Championship thanks to a superior goal difference over the Scots. It was a record 40th victory in the tournament for England.

Wolverhampton Wanderers stalwart Billy Wright achieved a personal milestone today in 1959 when he made his 100th appearance for England. Wright captained the England team at Wembley that beat Scotland 1-0 thanks to a Bobby Charlton goal. He was not only the first man to win 100 England caps, but the first player of any country to have reached 100 caps. His final total was 105 caps, 90 of which he was captain for – a record that still stands today. Tory peer Baron Brabazon of Tara saluted him: 'Not since Romulus and Remus has there been such a distinguished Wolf.'

APRIL 12

The old Wembley Stadium was already a fabled ground having hosted the White Horse FA Cup Final in 1923, but today in 1924 England played under the twin towers for the first time, with Scotland providing the opposition. Just to prove goalkeeping howlers at Wembley were happening long before Scott Carson was around, it was England's number one Teddy Taylor who gifted the opener to the Scots when Willie Cowen's shot hit Taylor's back and was deflected in. England equalised in the second half with a goal from Aston Villa striker Billy Walker and the game finished 1-1.

England hosted Scotland again on this day in 1947 at Wembley, and again the match ended in a 1-1 draw with goals from Sunderland's Raich Carter for England and Andy McLaren for Scotland. The result was enough for England to clinch the first Home Championship title since the end of the Second World War.

APRIL 13

England have lost twice to Scotland on this day in history. The first, in 1889, was played at the Kennington Oval where 10,000 fans saw England go down 3-2 to the Scots. Scotland's second goal was the 50th they had scored against England.

The second match was in 1929 at Hampden Park. Even with Dixie Dean in the side England could not score and it looked like the game would end as a 0-0 stalemate until the 89th minute when Alex Cheyne scored direct from a corner to win it. The unlikely feat had only been legalised the year before and it had never before happened in an England game. Cheyne reputedly managed to do it again twice in the same match in a Scottish Cup tie the following year. No England player has ever done it while on duty for the national side.

APRIL 14

England enjoyed one of their biggest wins over fierce rivals Scotland on this day when they trounced them 6-1 on their own patch in front of a full house at Hampden Park. Tommy Lawton got two, while Robert Brown, Raich Carter, Stanley Matthews and Leslie Smith got the others in a crushing win. Sadly, because the match was a wartime international played in 1945 it does not count as an official match between the two nations.

Eleven years earlier to the day and Horatio 'Raich' Carter made his England debut, also against Scotland, this time at Wembley Stadium. The Sunderland captain, who was the youngest man at the time to skipper his club to the First Division title, was a contemporary of Stanley Matthews and one of the greatest English pre-war players. Like so many of his generation he was robbed of many of his best years by the war but still won 13 official caps. He is also the only player to have won the FA Cup both before and after the Second World War with Sunderland and Preston respectively.

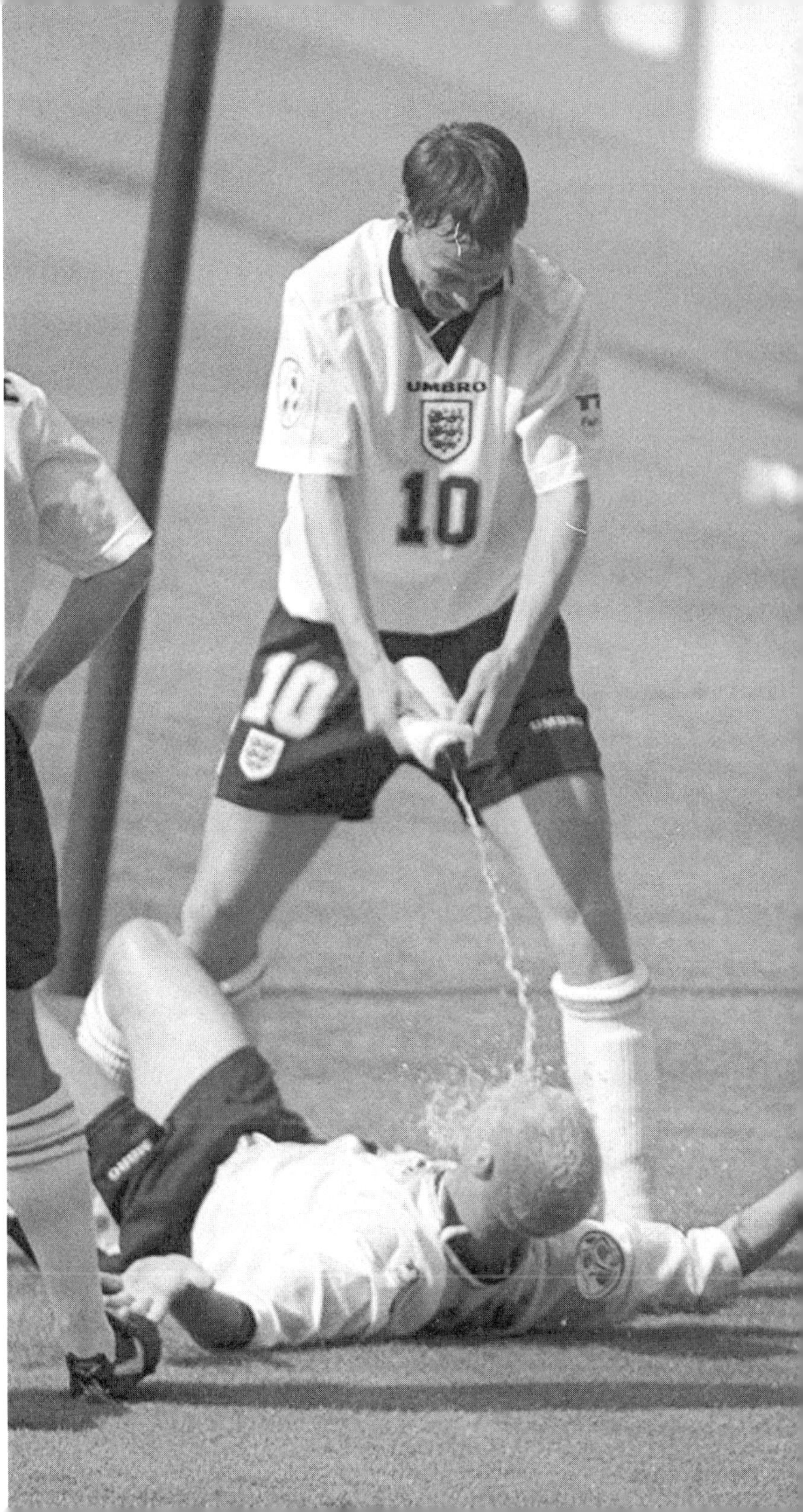

PAUL GASCOIGNE REPLICATES THE INFAMOUS 'DENTIST'S CHAIR' AFTER HIS SENSATIONAL GOAL AGAINST SCOTLAND IN EURO 96

APRIL 15

England went goal crazy on this day in 1961 when they inflicted Scotland's heaviest ever defeat at Wembley. A late withdrawal by regular Scottish keeper Bill Brown meant Celtic's Frank Haffey was between the sticks, but he needn't really have bothered as a Jimmy Greaves hat-trick, plus goals from Robert Smith, Johnny Haynes, Bryan Douglas and Bobby Robson saw England win 9-3. The joke soon doing the rounds was, 'What's the time at Wembley? Nine past Haffey!' Hilarious.

Scotland had their revenge today in 1967 when they came back to Wembley and became the first team to beat World Champions England since they lifted the Jules Rimet the previous year. After the 3-2 defeat Bobby Moore recalled: 'They went absolutely mad over it. The eyes of some of the players were wild. Their supporters came pouring off the terraces to cut up the pitch, waving lumps of earth at us and saying this was the turf on which they destroyed the world champions. Some of them were suggesting we ought to hand over the World Cup.'

APRIL 16

Malcolm Macdonald only ever played 14 times for England but today in 1975 he equalled an England scoring record when he bagged all five goals in a 5-0 win against Cyprus at Wembley. SuperMac was the last man to score five in an England shirt, but he never scored again for the Three Lions.

Michael Owen provided most of the goals during Sven-Göran Eriksson's England reign and today in 2002 Sven appointed him captain in David Beckham's absence for a friendly with Paraguay. Sven said: 'Michael was the best footballer in Europe last year and I think he's a very clean and popular one inside and outside England. It's up to him to show that he's also a leader and I think he is.'

APRIL 17

Michael Owen led the England team out as captain for the first time on this day in 2002. He took the armband for the friendly against Paraguay at Anfield. He was the second youngest England captain ever at 22 years and 124 days – only Bobby Moore skippered the side at a younger age. Owen led by example and scored the first goal after just three minutes in a 4-0 win over the Paraguayans.

England were on the wrong end of a 3-1 scoreline today in 1937 when they lost to Scotland at Hampden Park. Freddie Steele opened the scoring for England on 40 minutes but Frank O'Donnell and Bob McPhail netted for Scotland. The England players were wearing numbers on their shirts for the very first time and the near 150,000-strong crowd made this the highest-attended sporting event in British history. It was also the biggest for any international match until the opening of the Maracanã in Rio at the 1950 World Cup finals.

APRIL 18

While 'Three Lions' and 'World in Motion' are probably the most fondly remembered England songs, it was the team anthem for the 1970 World Cup, 'Back Home' that started the tradition. As reigning World Champions England had high hopes going into the tournament in Mexico and the whole squad recorded the song before they travelled. It reached number one in the UK singles chart on this day in 1970 and stayed there for three weeks.

World Cup songs were yet to be invented in 1942 when the horrors of war were more of a talking point than the Barnsey Rap. But there was still time for football and the 91,000 Scots who packed into Hampden Park were in for a treat today as Scotland beat England 5-4, with Bill Shankly on the scoresheet for the Scots.

APRIL 19

Just a few months after he had survived the Munich air crash, Bobby Charlton made his England debut on this day in 1958. The Manchester United forward was selected to face Scotland at Hampden Park alongside Billy Wright, Johnny Haynes and Tom Finney. Charlton set up the first goal, laying on a header for Bryan Douglas, and then scored the third himself – a trademark volley from a Finney cross. Scottish 'keeper Tommy Younger immediately rushed out to shake Charlton's hand before the restart, saying to him: 'Congratulations on your first game – and your first goal. There will be many more laddie.' The match finished 4-0. Charlton's goal was the first of 49 he scored for his country.

Brazil were the visitors to Wembley today in 1978 when they played England in a friendly match. Gil scored for Brazil after just nine minutes but England skipper Kevin Keegan rescued the day for the 90,000 fans when he netted the equaliser 20 minutes before the final whistle.

APRIL 20

Former England captain Ernie 'the fastest full-back in the west' Blenkinsop was born on this day in 1902. The long-time Sheffield Wednesday left-back made his international debut against France in 1928 and then played in every single England game for five years, never missing a match. His 26 consecutive matches was a record at the time.

When Fabio Capello was appointed England manager in 2008 he said the idea of the job had always fascinated him. Perhaps that was because on this day in 1999 he very nearly got the job. With Kevin Keegan employed as national boss on a temporary basis, the FA had to look abroad for a possible successor. Capello, who had already won four Serie A titles and the European Cup with AC Milan and La Liga with Real Madrid, met with Howard Wilkinson, then the FA's technical director about the job. In the end Keegan took the job full time, while the FA eventually got Capello nearly a decade later.

APRIL 21

With 49 England goals, Bobby Charlton was his country's record goalscorer until Wayne Rooney overtook him in 2015. Charlton got the 48th on this day in 1970 on his 100th appearance for his country. He got the last goal in a 3-1 win over Northern Ireland in the Home Championship at Wembley. Martin Peters opened the scoring after just six minutes. George Best equalised just after the re-start but Geoff Hurst and Charlton scored to win it for England. For Charlton, it was the 13th consecutive season he had scored for England.

Matthew Le Tissier only got eight caps for the full England side, despite being one of the most gifted players of his generation. Today in 1998 he played in an England B team match against Russia at Loftus Road. It was said to be his last chance to show Glenn Hoddle he had what it took to be in the France 98 World Cup squad. He played superbly, scoring a hat-trick and hitting the bar in a 4-1 win but he still did not go to the World Cup.

APRIL 22

Hampden Park was packed to the rafters today in 1944 when 133,000 fans squeezed in to watch a wartime international between Scotland and England. The majority of fans would have gone home unhappy though, as England won 3-2 thanks to two goals from Tommy Lawton and one from Horatio Carter.

Gary and Phil Neville made a little piece of history today in 1998 in a friendly match against Portugal at Wembley. Gary was in the starting line-up for the game which England comfortably won 3-0 with two goals from Alan Shearer and one from Teddy Sheringham, but in the second half Gary was replaced by his brother Phil. This is the only time an England player has been substituted for his brother.

APRIL 23

When the Home Championship was discontinued in 1984 it meant an end to the annual showdown between England and Scotland. The Rous Cup, named after former FA secretary and Fifa president Sir Stanley Rous, was the solution: a one match contest between the two auld enemies, which was later extended to include a guest South American team. It was held for the second time today in 1986 when goals from Glenn Hoddle and Terry Butcher gave England a 2-1 win.

Joey Barton only played once for England, with successive managers perhaps put off by his bad boy antics. He was in the dock, literally, today in 2008 when he appeared in court charged with assault occasioning actual bodily harm and affray after an incident outside a McDonald's in Liverpool on Boxing Day the previous year.

APRIL 24

England drew 2-2 with Scotland at Maine Road on this day in 1946. The match was organised to raise funds for the victims of the Burnden Park disaster of March of that year when 33 people died and hundreds more were injured in a crush at a match between Bolton and Stoke. At the time it was the worst disaster in British football history.

As manager of the all-conquering Leeds United team of the sixties and seventies, future England boss Don Revie was used to being handed awards. But he got a bit of a shock in 1974 when he was the surprise subject of the show *This is Your Life*, which was broadcast on this day. Host Eamonn Andrews surprised the 46-year-old Revie on Sunday, April 21, 1974 as he attended a Variety Club of Great Britain dinner at Leeds' Queens Hotel. His wife Elsie had known for three weeks that he was due to feature. She told the *Yorkshire Evening Post* at the time: 'Don was completely stunned, he had no idea at all.' The show was broadcast on the same night Leeds were confirmed as league champions by a defeat for their closest rivals Liverpool.

APRIL 25

The very first international football match between England and Scotland in 1872 ended in a 0-0 draw. It took nearly a whole century and 86 more games between the two teams to produce another scoreless draw. It finally happened on this day in 1970 when both Gordon Banks and Jim Cruikshank kept clean sheets in a Home Championship match at Hampden Park.

World Cup winner Alan Ball was also in the team that day for England. Today in 2007 he died aged 61 after he suffered a heart attack in his back garden. Sir Geoff Hurst, who scored England's third goal from Ball's cross in the World Cup final said: 'He was the youngest member of the team and man of the match in the 1966 World Cup final. Socially he was always a good laugh and the 1966 team mixed a lot after then. We are all totally devastated.'

APRIL 26

Despite being auld enemies, England and Scotland played out the friendliest of matches today in 1919. As the world tried to pick itself up after the First World War had ended, England took on Scotland in a Victory International match at Goodison Park. A crowd of 45,000 saw a 2-2 draw, but the match was one of the cleanest ever and only four free kicks were awarded in the whole 90 minutes. Robert Turnbull of Bradford Park Avenue and Sydney Puddefoot of West Ham United scored for England.

Paul Gascoigne put the icing on a five-goal win against Albania in a World Cup qualifier match today at Wembley in 1989. Peter Beardsley (2), Gary Lineker and Chris Waddle all netted for England before Gazza added the fifth with just two minutes remaining. It was his first international goal.

APRIL 27

Although Paul Ince was the first black captain of the full England side when he took the armband for a match against the United States in June 1993, he was not the first black man to captain England. That honour fell to former Aston Villa and Middlesbrough defender Ugo Ehiogu who skippered the England under-21 team on this day in 1993 against Holland under-21s at Portsmouth's Fratton Park ground.

With Sven-Göran Eriksson due to step down as England boss after the 2006 World Cup the FA were keen to appoint his successor before the tournament. Today in 2006 the FA chief executive offered the job to then Portugal manager Luiz Felipe Scolari. The Brazilian rejected the offer and the FA turned to Steve McClaren.

APRIL 28

Sir Alf Ramsey, the man who masterminded England's World Cup win in 1966, passed away on this day in 1999, aged 79. Sir Bobby Charlton said: 'I couldn't be more upset if it was family. Alf Ramsey gave all of us in the football business the greatest moment we have ever had as players, as coaches, as managers, as fans and as officials. He was professional to his fingertips and as popular with the players as any manager I've ever seen. He was a winner and without Alf Ramsey England would not have won the World Cup in 1966. He gave us our proudest moment.'

One of Sir Alf's successors as national team boss was Kevin Keegan. After answering England's SOS call after Glenn Hoddle's abrupt departure, KK initially said he would only manage the team for four games. After taking charge of an England friendly away at Hungary, Keegan admitted he wanted to stay longer. 'Now, having done it for two games, I really feel I belong here,' he said. 'It's time to stop playing games, I want the job.'

APRIL 29

Two years after their heartbreaking defeat to West Germany in the 1970 World Cup, England had the chance for some revenge on this day in 1972 when they took on their old foes at Wembley in a European Championship quarter-final match. Sadly, England were not the team they had been in Mexico while the West Germans had got better. Günter Netzer played the starring role in midfield for the visitors who simply destroyed England. Where two years earlier it had been a dramatic and close sporting contest, this was simply a stronger beast overpowering its prey. Goals from Uli Hoeneß and Gerd Müller plus a later penalty from Netzer ensured West Germany won 3-1.

England's goal that day came from Manchester City's Franny Lee – he turned 28 that day and is still the last England player to score for his country on his birthday, but it was the last time he ever played for England.

APRIL 30

He had led England to World Cup glory but in football no one is indispensable and today in 1973 it was announced that Sir Alf Ramsey had been sacked as England manager. It followed England's failure to qualify for the 1974 World Cup and a clash of personalities between Sir Alf and FA bigwig Sir Harold Thompson. The decision to replace Ramsey was taken on April 2 but it was not made public until today. Even Sir Alf had no idea until April 21 when he was summoned to Lancaster Gate to receive the news. In Dave Bowler's biography of Ramsey, *Winning Isn't Everything*, Sir Alf is quoted: 'It was the most devastating half-hour of my life. I stood in a room almost full of staring committee men. It was just like I was on trial. I thought I was going to be hanged. Typically I was never given one reason for the sack.'

ENGLAND
ON THIS DAY

MAY

MAY 1

Pint-sized agitator Dennis Wise marked his first England appearance with the winning goal against Turkey today in 1991. Also making his debut in England's 1-0 Euro 92 qualifying win in Izmir was Crystal Palace midfielder Geoff Thomas as he made the first of his nine England appearances. Following his retirement from football Thomas was diagnosed with leukaemia from which he later recovered and has since established a charity that organised the first game at the new Wembley Stadium in 2007, when the Geoff Thomas Foundation Charity XI took on a team of celebrities.

When Fabio Capello quit as England boss just four months before Euro 2012, Harry Redknapp was the overwhelming favourite to get the job. But on this day the FA went with the far safer option of then-West Brom boss Roy Hodgson. A quarter-final defeat to Italy that year was the high point of Hodgson's reign, which ended with that 2-1 loss to Iceland four years later.

MAY 2

Wales recorded their last victory over England today in 1984 when Mark Hughes bagged the only goal in a Home Championship clash at the Racecourse Ground. Making their debuts for England that day were Mark Wright and Terry Fenwick, but none of them would get a chance to avenge the defeat, as the Home Championship was discontinued that year and it would be 20 years until they met again, with England doing the double over the Dragons in the 2006 World Cup qualifying campaign.

It's happy birthday to perhaps the planet's most famous player since Pele, as former England skipper David Beckham was born today in 1975. Goldenballs' England career has featured more highs and lows than most, hitting rock bottom with his red card against Argentina in 1998 then rebuilding his career with the best comeback since Lazarus by slotting home *that* free kick against Greece to secure qualification for the 2002 World Cup.

MAY 3

England and Scotland replayed their match that was called off following the first Ibrox disaster today in 1902. A month earlier 26 fans had died and 587 were injured after the newly built West Tribune Stand at Ibrox collapsed due to heavy rainfall the previous night. The re-arranged game took place at Villa Park, with the proceeds going to the disaster fund, as the sides drew 2-2.

England and Scotland contested a Victory International today in 1919 and treated the 80,000 that packed into Hampden Park to a thriller, as England almost threw away a three goal half-time lead on their way to a 4-3 win. Arthur Grimsdell of Tottenham and West Ham's Sydney Puddefoot both scored twice for the Three Lions.

MAY 4

'Manifestly out of his depth, the very embodiment of the Peter Principle, whereby people are constantly promoted one step above their capacities.' This was how football doyen Brian Glanville welcomed the Steve McClaren era which started today in 2006 when the FA named the hapless Yorkshireman as Sven's post-World Cup replacement. After a farcical four-month appointment process, where 'Big' Phil Scolari had very publicly turned down the FA's overtures, the suits at Soho Square gave the Middlesbrough boss a four-year contract, despite the selection committee only recommending a two-year deal. FA chief executive Brian Barwick put on his best poker face and said: 'My first choice was always Steve. That might be difficult for people to get their heads across.'

Back on the pitch in 1966 Alf Ramsey was putting the finishing touches to the Three Lions' World Cup preparations as England faced Yugoslavia at Wembley. First-half goals from Jimmy Greaves and Bobby Charlton secured a routine 2-0 win in front of 55,000 fans. Making his debut that day was Martin Peters, who would end the summer scoring in the World Cup final.

MAY 5

With the Nazis about to surrender in Western Europe, England went to Wales for their final wartime international today in 1945. As was the norm for these unrecognised games goals weren't in short supply, with England triumphing 3-2 thanks to a Horatio Carter hat-trick. The Derby and Sunderland striker was one of an unlucky group of England players that saw their best years go unrecognised, as the games played during both the world wars were unofficial in the eyes of Fifa.

Today in 1965 England finally got the chance to extract a small amount of revenge on the Mighty Magyars of Hungary that had humiliated them in 1953 and '54. Jimmy Greaves scored the only goal as Alf Ramsey's men won 1-0 in a friendly at Wembley.

MAY 6

One of European football's oft-overlooked greats tore England apart today in 1936, as Matthias Sindelar inspired Austria to a 2-1 win over England in Vienna. Known as 'the Mozart of football', Sindelar was the focal point of visionary coach Hugo Meisl's Austrian 'Wunderteam' of the 1920s and '30s. Sindelar refused to play for Germany when Austria was annexed by the Nazis in 1938 and was tragically found dead with his girlfriend in January 1939. The official verdict found carbon monoxide poisoning to be the cause, but conspiracy theorists have pointed to either suicide or murder by Nazi officials.

Bobby Charlton notched up his 50th cap today in 1964 as the Three Lions took on Uruguay at Wembley. Two goals from West Ham striker Johnny 'Budgie' Byrne gave England a 2-1 win in a game that saw World Cup winner George Cohen make his England bow. Cohen's nephew Ben would go on to lift the Webb Ellis Cup with the England rugby union team in 2003, giving the family a unique World Cup winning double.

MAY 7

Although the penalty shoot-out wouldn't be introduced for another 12 years, the warning signs were there for England today in 1958 when Jim Langley missed a second-half penalty against Portugal, hitting the post. This was England's fifth consecutive spot-kick miss at Wembley and the national psyche was already starting to bear those spot-kick scars. Luckily for Langley, Bobby Charlton was on hand to bag a brace in a 2-1 win.

Fast forward 11 years to 1969 and what were England doing? You guessed it, missing another penalty. This time the Three Lions were taking on Wales and it was the turn of Franny Lee to lose his bottle from the Wembley penalty spot. He did, however, make up for it scoring England's winner in a 2-1 victory that featured the debut of West Brom legend and *Fantasy Football League* favourite Jeff Astle.

MAY 8

Jack Charlton was well-known for his little black book where he'd keep a note of all those players that he felt needed a spot of 'extra attention' next time he met, but today in 1973 he was presented with the big red book as he featured on BBC's *This Is Your Life* on his 38th birthday. Contained within its pages will have been details of his 35 England caps and 773 appearances for Leeds, which remains their club record.

FA bosses made one of their rare wise decisions today in 1963 when they handed Ipswich Town manager Alf Ramsey the England job that been vacant since Walter Winterbottom had left the role after England's game with Wales in November 1962. At Ipswich Ramsey had guided the Tractor Boys from the Third Division South right to the top, winning the Division 1 title in 1962 in his eight-year spell at Portman Road.

May 9

Bernard Joy became the last amateur to play for England today in 1936 when he took the field against Belgium at Heysel in Brussels. Bernard's joy was short-lived though as England suffered a surprise 3-2 loss and the Causals centre-half never turned out again for the Three Lions.

Another first today in 1962 when Gerry Hitchens of Internazionale stepped out against the Swiss at Wembley, becoming the first player to represent England whilst at an overseas club. He scored the second goal in a 3-1 win for England, but his career would stall when Alf Ramsey took charge of the dugout, as he preferred to select home-based players. Making his 20th and final appearance for his country that day was Bobby Robson, who would return as manager in 1982.

May 10

As the rest of the football world prepared for a World Cup that England thought they were too good for, the Three Lions took on Germany for the first time today in 1930. England needed a late David Jack equaliser to secure a 3-3 draw after German striker Richard Hofmann scored a hat-trick. England were forced to play the second half with only ten men after left-half William Marsden suffered a horrific spinal injury shortly before the break which would end his career. Birmingham City's Joe Bradford had scored England's other two goals as one of international football's most intense rivalries was up and running.

England's leading goalscorer Bobby Charlton was in rampant mood today in 1961 as he bagged a hat-trick in an emphatic 8-0 win over Mexico at Wembley. Aston Villa striker Gerry Hitchens marked his debut with a goal in the second minute and joining him on the scoresheet were Bobby Robson, Ron Flowers and Bryan Douglas who bagged a brace.

MAY 11

Joe Mercer took charge of England for the first time today in 1974, as the Three Lions took on Wales in a Home Championship match at Ninian Park. Mercer gave a debut to Kevin Keegan, who repaid the new gaffer with second-half goal to add to eccentric QPR striker Stan Bowles' opener, which would prove to be his only international goal.

Dixie Dean is widely considered to be one of the game's all-time great finishers and this was evident when he stuck three past Belgium today in 1927. England thrashed the Flemish 9-1 in Brussels and Dean would go on to bag another hat-trick in his next game against Luxembourg ten days later – the only time a player has scored successive trebles for England, as the Everton striker was on his way to 12 goals in his first five England appearances.

MAY 12

Gordon Banks earned undoubtedly the easiest of his 73 caps today in 1971, touching the ball only four times against Malta at Wembley – and they were all back-passes. England won their European Championship qualifier 5-0, with Martin Chivers setting the tone early, scoring in the first minute. Chris Lawler made a goalscoring debut and the rout was completed by strikes from Franny Lee, Alan Clarke and a second from Chivers.

England beat the Germans for the fifth consecutive time today in 1965, when they took on Helmut Schon's men in Nuremberg. A solitary goal from Southampton's Terry Paine was enough to defeat the old enemy in a match that saw Everton's Derek Temple win his only cap and Mick Jones – of Leeds United, not the Clash – make his debut.

MAY 13

Walter Winterbottom took his England team to the Maracanã in Rio today in 1959 to take on the World Champions Brazil. With over 160,000 packed into the famous stadium the game remains the record attendance for an England match. Goals from Julinho and Henrique ensured that the masses went home happy, celebrating a 2-0 win for the South Americans.

England faced another old rival in 1972 as they took on West Germany in the European Championship quarter-finals second leg. Having suffered a 3-1 reverse at Wembley two weeks earlier England were unable to break their opponents down in Berlin, drawing 0-0. West Germany would then go on to win the tournament, defeating the USSR 3-0 in the final.

MAY 14

One of the most infamous incidents in the history of the England team occurred today in 1938 when they took on Germany in Berlin. As captain Eddie Hapgood and his players lined up for the pre-match ceremonies they issued a Nazi salute to the crowd. The FA wanted to comply with the Foreign Office's policy of appeasement and deemed the salute necessary, with Stan Cullis later insisting that the players were forced into it: 'We were informed in a diplomatic way that if we didn't give the salute we wouldn't be selected for future England games.' The result, a 6-3 win to England, has gone down in history as little more than a footnote.

One of the defining moments of the 1966 World Cup win was Kenneth Wolstenholme's legendary commentary. However, earlier that summer the BBC man was feeling rather coy. When Everton beat Sheffield Wednesday in today's FA Cup final thanks to a late brace from Mike Trebilcock, Wolstenholme refused to say the word 'cock', instead referring to him as 'Trebilco'. Luckily, his famous phrase that greeted Geoff Hurst's hat-trick six weeks later is the one that has gone down in history.

MAY 15

One of England's greats bowed out today in 1957, when Stanley Matthews made his final appearance for his country at the grand old age of 42. England were taking on Denmark in Copenhagen, with Matthews helping the Three Lions to a 4-1 win in his 54th cap. Matthews would have surely broken all kinds of England records had his career not been interrupted by World War II, but he remains the oldest player to turn out for England. He would go on playing top-flight football until he was 50 years old and picked up a Knighthood in 1965, whilst still running the wings at Stoke.

England could have done with Sir Stan in 1929, as they slumped to a shock 4-3 defeat to an up-and-coming Spanish side in Madrid. *The Daily Express* was in shell-shock, writing: 'I never thought I would live to see the day when 11 Spanish players humbled the might – more or less – of English soccer.' Whilst the result has not gone down in history with the same significance of Hungary's 1953 win over England, this was perhaps the first time that England's belief in their pre-ordained right to be the best in the world at the game they invented was shaken.

MAY 16

England took on Italy in Turin today in 1948 and ever since the 'Battle of Highbury' 14 years earlier relations between the two had been frosty to say the least. England cantered to a 4-0 win and Stanley Matthews did his best to wind up the Azzurri by showboating his way to the corner flag in the second half, where he paused, smoothed his hair with a comb, and then sent in a cross. Even David Beckham's never been vain enough to do his hair whilst actually *on* the ball.

World Cup hero Alan Ball notched up his first England goal today in 1965 when he opened the scoring against Sweden in Gothenburg's Ullevi Stadion. England would go on to win 2-1, with Manchester United's John Connelly netting the winner. The Three Lions would go one better in 2018, beating the Swedes 2-0 in the World Cup quarter-final in Russia.

May 17

A Johnny Byrne hat-trick helped England to a 4-3 win over Portugal in Lisbon today in 1964. Making his debut that day was Liverpool winger Peter Thompson, who can lay a claim to being one of the unluckiest England players ever. The man dubbed 'the white Pelé' during that summer's visit to Brazil was in the provisional squads for the 1966 and 1970 World Cups, but missed the cut both times as Alf Ramsey's 'wingless wonders' had no place for Thompson's talent on the flanks.

Today in 1975 saw Ramsey's successor Don Revie's sixth game in charge and with it a sixth consecutive clean sheet as England drew 0-0 with Northern Ireland at Windsor Park in Belfast.

May 18

Today's FA Cup Final in 1991 was one of those *Sliding Doors* moments for the English football team. Paul Gascoigne had followed up his swashbuckling Italia 90 campaign with another excellent season and began Spurs' match against Nottingham Forest like a man possessed, first planting his studs on Garry Parker's chest then scything down Gary Charles after only 15 minutes. After joining the Spurs wall for the resulting free kick Gazza crumpled into a mess on the floor, having torn his cruciate knee ligament. England teammate and Gazza's opponent that day Stuart Pearce later wrote: 'That wild tackle had a massive effect on his career. He was never quite the same player afterwards.'

More England woe today in 1970 as an innocent trip into a Bogotá jewellers turned into an international incident. Bobbies Moore and Charlton were shopping for a gift for the Manchester United man's wife and as they left the shop the owner called the police, claiming Moore had pocketed a diamond bracelet. After being placed under house arrest for two weeks the case was dropped when it emerged that the tracksuit Moore was wearing did not have any pockets, meaning Moore could join up with his team in Mexico in time for their first World Cup match against Brazil.

MAY 19

Four years earlier Stuart Pearce was an electrician and plumber that played non-league football for Wealdstone, but today in 1987 he must have been pinching himself as he lined up for England at Wembley Stadium to play Brazil in front of 92,000 fans for his international debut. Goals from Gary Lineker and Mirandinha ensured a 1-1 draw in this opening Rous Cup match and the South Americans would go on to lift the trophy.

Any latecomers were punished for their tardiness when England took on Portugal today in 1951 at Goodison Park, as both sides scored in the first minute. Bill Nicholson scored after 30 seconds on his England debut, but his joy was short-lived when Demetrico Patalino equalised immediately after. Three goals in the last 15 minutes gave England a 5-2 win in front of 52,686 fans.

MAY 20

Bobby Moore made his England debut today in 1962 as the Three Lions took on Peru in Lima. The 21-year-old helped England to a 4-0 win over the South Americans, with Moore's good friend and drinking buddy Jimmy Greaves grabbing a hat-trick. Moore would go to make another 107 appearances for the Three Lions, securing his place in England footballing immortality in the summer of 1966.

Bolton legend Nat Lofthouse broke Steve Bloomer's 49-year-old scoring record when he fired home his 29th England goal against Finland today in 1956. His 63rd minute strike at the Olympiastadion in Helsinki was England's 900th goal as the Finns were crushed 5-1.

MAY 21

The Fédération Internationale de Football – or Fifa to it's friends – was formed today in 1904, but England initially showed little interest in Robert Guérin's brainchild, believing themselves to be above that sort of thing. The FA showing it's usual decisiveness joined the fold a year later as they attempted to use the organisation to impose their rules as the worldwide standard, but left ten years later when the First World War broke out. England and the rest of the home nations eventually returned in 1946, having missed out on the first three World Cups.

Had England stayed away from Fifa and the World Cup we would never have been subjected to some of the god-awful World Cup songs that are now tradition. However, the 1990 version was the exception that proves the rule, as New Order, with a little help from John Barnes, today released 'World In Motion'. Co-written by actor and comedian Keith 'Lily's dad' Allen, the song featured several squad members including Paul Gascoigne on backing vocals, but is most fondly remembered for Barnes spitting out lyrics such as: 'Catch me if you can/Cos I'm the England man/And what you're looking at/Is the master plan.'

MAY 22

England warmed up for the 1990 World Cup by taking on Uruguay today in a friendly at Wembley Stadium. A disappointing 2-1 loss on Gary Lineker's 50th appearance meant that the knives were out for Bobby Robson before the squad departed to Italy for the tournament.

Argentina were the South American visitors today in 1974, but failure in their 1974 World Cup qualification campaign meant that England had less to play for than their opponents that day. England threw away a two-goal lead, with Mario Kempes scoring twice, including a last minute penalty, to draw 2-2.

MAY 23

In 1954 England travelled to Budapest intent on revenge following their humiliation against the Mighty Magyars of Hungary six months earlier. Instead, England were again undone by Puskás, Hidegkuti and company, suffering a 7-1 defeat which remains their biggest ever loss.

In 1989 perhaps England fans were fearful of a repeat performance, as only 15,628 turned up at Wembley to watch the Rous Cup clash with Chile. This is England's lowest ever Wembley attendance, due mainly to a tube strike, but those that did bother probably wish they didn't as the two sides played out a 0-0 draw in a match that featured John Fashanu and Nigel Clough's England debuts.

MAY 24

England's penalty hoodoo didn't actually begin when Stuart Pearce and Chris Waddle failed from the spot against West Germany in 1990, as the England women's squad began the trend in the European Championship final today in 1984. This time Sweden were the opponents as England's women lost 4-3 on penalties at Luton Town's Kenilworth Road. In the squad that day was the current national team coach Hope Powell, but it was Linda Curl that missed the vital spot-kick. Curl had hit 22 goals in a 40-0 win for Norwich against Milton Keynes Reserves a year earlier, but could not find a way past Swedish 'keeper Elisabeth Leidinge and a national jinx was born.

Meanwhile in Sheffield that very same day England's under-21 team went one better as they defeated Spain to win the European Championships. Going into the tournament as defending champions, the youngsters were inspired by Mark Hateley who bagged the opener, following his four-goal performance against France in the quarter-finals. Howard Gayle scored a second, as England secured a 3-0 aggregate win.

MAY 25

Tommy Lawton wasted no time in getting stuck into Portugal today in 1947, as he struck after just 17 seconds, clocking up England's fastest-ever goal. Debutant Stan Mortensen wasn't far behind though, scoring in the second minute as England romped to a 10-0 win in Lisbon. The pair ended up with four goals apiece in one of England's easier away-days.

Another routine win followed in 2001 as Sven-Göran Eriksson's men took on Mexico in a friendly at Derby's Pride Park. With England cruising 3-0 at half-time Svennis did his party-trick of making ten substitutions, handing debuts to West Ham pair Joe Cole and Michael Carrick and Leeds duo Alan Smith and Danny Mills. England ended up with a 4-0 win with Scholes, Fowler, Beckham and Sheringham all getting on the scoresheet.

MAY 26

To this day his teammates and contemporaries insist that Duncan Edwards was destined to become one of England's greats before his life was tragically cut short in the Munich air disaster and that is largely due to performances like the one he put in today in 1956 against West Germany. Inspiring the Three Lions to a 3-1 win in Berlin, he scored the first goal after surging past three defenders and smashing the ball home from 30 yards. His captain that day, Billy Wright, said: 'There have been few individual performances to match what he produced that day. Duncan tackled like a lion, attacked at every opportunity and topped it off with a cracker of a goal.'

Making his debut today in 1984 was another England legend, Gary Lineker. The Leicester City striker came on as a 72nd minute substitute in England's Home Championship match against Scotland at Hampden Park. Although the crisp enthusiast failed to trouble the scoresheet that afternoon, he would go on to bag 48 goals for his country, agonisingly one short of Bobby Charlton's then-record.

MAY 27

It's happy birthday to Gazza today, and on the occasion of his 27th in 1996 the England squad partied like... well, like it was Gazza's birthday. On a pre-Euro 96 trip to Hong Kong the team hit the nightclubs hard, ending up in the infamous 'dentist's chair', where they took it in turns to pour booze down each other's necks. The flight home afterwards proved to be equally raucous as two televisions got smashed, along with a number of arm rests, when, according to reports, a sleeping Dennis Wise fell out of an overhead locker after teammates had stashed him away. The dentist's chair shenanigans would provide Gazza with his most famous on-field celebration later that summer.

Alan Ball was also upsetting the natives today in 1972, when England took on the Scots at Hampden Park. As he prepared to take a corner he wiped his nose on the corner flag, which bore the St Andrew's Cross. With the 119,325 crowd baying for his blood, Ball had the last laugh, scoring the only goal of the match. Adding fumes to the fire, Alf Ramsey found the whole incident highly amusing, saying: 'Alan, Alan, you really are a very naughty boy.'

MAY 28

Bowing out today in 1959 was legendary England defender Billy Wright. Winning his 105th cap and 90th as captain, Wright made his final appearance against the USA in Los Angeles. Wright was able to put to bed any lingering memories of the humiliating 1950 loss as England cruised to an 8-1 win, thanks to a seven-goal second half from the English, including a Bobby Charlton hat-trick.

England were back in the USA in 2005, with Sven's men winning 2-1 at Soldier Field in Chicago. Manchester United midfielder Kieran Richardson bagged both goals, as he made his debut alongside fellow new boys Zat Knight and Luke Young.

MAY 29

Bobby Moore donned the captain's armband for the first time today in 1963, becoming England's youngest ever skipper at the age of 22, as the Three Lions took on Czechoslovakia in Bratislava. The 22-year-old West Ham centre-back led his teammates to a 4-2 win with Jimmy Greaves grabbing two goals. Moore would go on to captain his country 90 times, equalling the record set by Billy Wright.

One of England's lesser-known penalty shoot-out losses came today in 1998, at the King Hussain II Tournament in Casablanca. Facing Belgium in a World Cup warm-up, the two sides drew 0-0 and underwent a shoot-out after 90 minutes. This time it was Rob Lee and 'Sir' Les Ferdinand that couldn't convert from 12 yards, as England gave their supporters a sneak preview of how that summer would end.

MAY 30

Most friendlies during the Sven era were pointless, dull affairs, but the World Cup warm-up against Hungary today in 2006 provided plenty to mull on. Making his debut as a second-half substitute was 17-year-old Theo Walcott who became the youngest-ever England player, as Sven eyed up the former Southampton youngster for a controversial place in his World Cup squad. John Terry chipped in with his first goal for the national team and Frank Lampard missed a penalty shortly before half-time. Liverpool duo Steven Gerrard and Peter Crouch both netted to give England a 3-1 win.

In 1981 the ugly side of English football reared its head, when travelling supporters rioted in Basle following England's 2-1 loss to Switzerland. A Swiss police chief said: 'If they are not seen here again for 50 years, it will be too soon.'

MAY 31

Ron Greenwood's side were Down Under today in 1980, taking on Australia. Goals from Glenn Hoddle and Paul Mariner gave England a 2-1 win in a game that featured the shortest-ever England career. Brighton & Hove Albion striker Peter Ward replaced fellow one-cap wonder Alan Sunderland in the 85th minute and never added to the five minutes he spent running around the Sydney Cricket Ground in England colours. Still, at least he got a trip to Australia out of it...

England captain Tony Adams scored what would be England's last-ever goal at the old Wembley Stadium today in 2000 in a 2-0 friendly win over Ukraine. As Steven Gerrard and Gareth Barry made their international debuts, Robbie Fowler got the opener and Kevin Keegan's men were unable to find the back of the net in their next, and final, game at the famous old stadium against Germany later that year.

ENGLAND
ON THIS DAY

JUNE

JUNE 1

Despite playing a crucial role in helping England qualify for the 1998 World Cup, today manager Glenn Hoddle decided not to include Paul Gascoigne in his squad for the tournament. In his World Cup diary book Hoddle recalled: 'He had snapped. He was ranting, swearing and slurring his words. He was acting like a man possessed. He seemed to be dealing with it quite well… then he stopped, turned and flew into a rage, kicking a nearby chair. It was a full-blooded volley and I was concerned because he had bare feet. The kick was so hard I thought he must have broken his foot. He was a different person now. He had snapped. I stood there and he turned as if to go again, then came back with a barrage of abuse.' Gazza never played for England again.

After seven years leading a nomadic existence, England returned to Wembley on this day in 2007 for the first match in the new stadium – a friendly against Brazil. Captain John Terry scored after 68 minutes to give England the lead but Ribas Diego equalised in the dying moments to rob England of a first win back at Wembley.

JUNE 2

England faced Argentina for the first time in a competitive match on this day in 1962 at the group stage of the World Cup in Chile. Goals from Ron Flowers, Jimmy Greaves and Bobby Charlton gave England a 3-1 win.

England drew 1-1 with Iceland in a friendly on this day in 1982 with a goal from substitute Paul Goddard. It was the only cap he ever won and his 50 minutes of play make his the shortest England career of any scorer. The match was supposed to be an England B game but Iceland wanted the game designated as a full international. The England A team played Finland the following day making it the first time England played matches on successive days since the early 1890s.

JUNE 3

Future England captain John Terry made his England debut on this day in 2003 as a second half substitute in a friendly against Serbia and Montenegro at the Walkers Stadium in Leicester. The only player left on the pitch at the final whistle who had started the match was England 'keeper David James and the 21 substitutions made is an international record. The England captaincy changed hands four times during the game; Michael Owen, Jamie Carragher, Phil Neville and Emile Heskey all took the armband.

Unlikely-looking England striker Peter Crouch was leading the line for his country today in 2006 in a friendly against Jamaica at Old Trafford. Despite missing a penalty Crouch still bagged a hat-trick and debuted the famous robot dance that made him a cult hero. England eventually won 6-0 which was the biggest win of Sven-Goran Eriksson's reign.

JUNE 4

They came, they saw, they conquered. And then they trashed the place. Scotland beat England 2-1 at Wembley today in 1977 to win the Home Championship thanks to goals from Gordon McQueen and Kenny Dalglish. After the final whistle the Tartan Army invaded the pitch and caused carnage, including snapping the crossbar of one of the goals. Kevin Keegan said: 'They looted the goalposts and the crossbars, the nets and the corner flags. They whipped out dirks from their kilts and cut out the penalty spots for souvenirs, then they began carving up keepsake patches of turf. Almost the only things left were the twin towers.'

Needing one last friendly before Euro 88, Bobby Robson's England took on Aylesbury United today in 1988 – the only time the full England side have ever played a non-league team. The plucky underdogs were beaten 7-0 in front of 6,000 fans squeezed into their Buckingham Road ground.

JUNE 5

England took on Yugoslavia on this day in 1968 in the semi-final of the European Championships in Italy. England lost 1-0 after a late goal by Dragan Džajić but Alan Mullery became the first England player to be sent off, in the last minute of the game. In the other semi, before the advent of penalty shoot-outs, Italy beat the USSR with a coin toss after a goalless draw.

Yugoslavia were again England's opponents in a friendly match on this day in 1974. The England team arrived directly in Yugoslavia from their previous match in Bulgaria and in Kevin Keegan's words were 'wearing casuals instead of uniforms and feeling in a jovial mood'. No officials were there to meet them at the airport and after some players were mucking around on the baggage belt, Keegan was hauled off to a back room by security guards where he was charged with sexually assaulting a stewardess, assaulting a security guard, disturbing the peace and causing an obstruction and then beaten up before FA officials could intervene. Keegan, by now in tears, was released and the charges then dropped. In the match, he scored England's second goal to equalise after 75 minutes.

JUNE 6

Just a year after England's World Cup semi-final defeat, there was more semis heartbreak for the Three Lions on this day in 2019 when an extra-time defensive horror show saw Gareth Southgate's men crash out of the Nations League with a 3-1 loss to the Netherlands.

Ray Wilkins became the first England player to see red at a World Cup today in 1986 when he was sent off for a second bookable offence when he threw the ball at Paraguayan referee Gabriel Gonzalez after being called offside during a laboured 0-0 draw against Morocco in the group stage. Wilkins came on as a sub in a World Cup qualifier away to Hungary today in 1981, but Trevor Brooking grabbed the headlines when he scored England's third in a 3-1 win. His left-footed shot from the edge of the area was so hard it got stuck in the stanchion.

JUNE 7

The reigning World Champions England versus the pre-tournament favourites Brazil was the mouth-watering match today at the 1970 World Cup in Mexico. Pele thought he had opened the scoring with a bullet header and was already shouting 'GOAL!' when Gordon Banks flung himself at the ball and pulled off one of the greatest saves of all time. Pele said: 'At that moment I hated Gordon Banks more than any man in soccer. But when I cooled down I had to applaud him with my heart for the greatest save I have ever seen.' Captain Bobby Moore, who made one of the best tackles ever seen against Jairzinho, told Banks afterwards: 'You're getting old Banksy, you used to hold on to those.' A Jairzinho goal gave Brazil a 1-0 win in one of the all-time classic matches.

England faced Argentina at the 2002 World Cup on this day, and captain David Beckham secured personal and national revenge for the defeat four years earlier by blasting a penalty to win it 1-0. 'It is a fantastic feeling. This is probably the sweetest moment of my whole career,' he said afterwards.

JUNE 8

Three years after the humiliating 1-0 defeat by the part-timers of the USA in the 1950 World Cup, England travelled to the States to take them on again in a friendly on this day in 1953 at Yankee Stadium. It was the first match England ever played under floodlights and two goals each from Tom Finney and Nat Lofthouse helped the Three Lions to a 6-3 win.

England took on Brazil in a friendly in Rio today in 1977 but forgot to take their socks and had to borrow blue socks from the hosts. The game was a 0-0 draw but for the first time there were eight past, present or future England captains in the team: Ray Clemence, Phil Neal, Trevor Cherry, Dave Watson, Emlyn Hughes, Kevin Keegan, Ray Wilkins and Mick Channon all played.

JUNE 9

Paul Ince made history today in 1993 when he became the first black player to captain the full England side. With regular skippers David Platt and Tony Adams missing and Ince in fine form for Manchester United, manager Graham Taylor gave him the armband for the friendly defeat to the USA in Massachusetts.

Remarkably, England won a second consecutive penalty shootout on this day in 2019. A 6-5 spot-kick win over Switzerland in Portugal meant their inaugural Nations League campaign ended with a third-placed finish.

JUNE 10

Jimmy Greaves showed his Dr Doolittle side during a World Cup quarter-final against Brazil on this day in 1962. England lost the match 3-1 after goals from Garrincha and Vava but during the game a stray dog ran on to the pitch and evaded everyone until Greavsie got down on all fours and beckoned the canine. He then grabbed the pooch who promptly urinated all over him. 'I smelt so bad, but at least it meant the Brazilian defenders stayed clear of me,' he said. Garrincha thought the whole thing was hilarious and kept the dog as a pet.

England faced Brazil again on this day in 1984. Bobby Robson's team had failed to reach the Euro 84 finals but a young John Barnes gave fans hope for the future when he out-Brazilled Brazil with one of the best goals ever scored by England. He picked up the ball on the left wing and took it past almost the entire Brazil defence before slotting past the goalkeeper. England won 2-0 – the first time Brazil had been beaten at the Maracanã for 27 years. Barnes said later: 'I don't remember much about my goal – I always liken it to an out-of-body experience. I look at it on TV now and I can't remember doing any of it.'

JUNE 11

England faced Czechoslovakia today at the 1970 World Cup in their final group match. Bobby Charlton's 105th cap matched the record set by former England captain Billy Wright. Bobby couldn't score but England debutant Allan Clarke scored in his first international match to secure a 1-0 win. Clarke became only the second man to score a penalty on his England debut after Tommy Lawton in 1938.

There wasn't much noteworthy about England's dull and dismal goalless draw with Denmark in their first match of Euro 92 on this day. The only point of interest from the bore-fest was that the England players wore shirts with their names on the back for the first time.

JUNE 12

A friendly against Argentina on this day in 1977 proved anything but when England's Trevor Cherry clashed with Daniel Bertoni. Cherry felled the Argentine with a tackle from behind and Bertoni threw a retaliatory punch that knocked out two of Cherry's teeth. Referee Ramon Barreto sent them both off, making this the only England game to see two red cards.

England's opening match at Euro 2000 was entirely predictable given that Kevin Keegan was in charge of the team. Paul Scholes and Steve McManaman gave England an early two goal lead with just 17 minutes played, but Luis Figo and Pinto pulled two back for Portugal before the break. Nuno Gomes scored the winner for Portugal on 60 minutes to cap an impressive comeback. KK said: 'You go 2-0 up and you've got to fancy your chances of going on to win. It is not the result I wanted but we will have to take it on the chin.'

JUNE 13

Between the 1990 and 2002 World Cups, the England goalkeeping jersey was generally the sole preserve of David Seaman. On the rare occasions the Arsenal stopper was not between the sticks, Tim Flowers often filled in. He made his debut on this day in 1993 when England played out a 1-1 draw with Brazil in the USA.

England and France began their Euro 2004 campaigns on this day in a highly anticipated match in the Estadio da Luz in Portugal. Frank Lampard gave England a 1-0 lead after 38 minutes, scoring a header from a Beckham cross. Wayne Rooney was looking superb in his first tournament match and won a penalty in the second half but Beckham saw his spot kick saved by Fabien Barthez. It got even worse for England in injury time when Zinedine Zidane curled in a brilliant free kick, before breaking England hearts with a penalty two minutes later.

JUNE 14

Today in 1970 was the day England lost the World Cup they had won four years earlier. In the quarter-final of the 1970 tournament in Mexico, England faced West Germany, the team they had beaten at Wembley in 1966. At first, everything went to plan as Alan Mullery and Martin Peters gave England a two goal lead. Then Beckenbauer pulled one back and then, thinking the match was won, Sir Alf Ramsey took off Bobby Charlton to save him for the semi-final that England would never reach. Uwe Seeler scored to take the match to extra time and with all the momentum with the Germans, Gerd Müller scored the winner. England were out, and so was Charlton. His record-breaking 106th cap was also his last.

Another day, another World Cup defeat for England, who lost on this day in 2014 to Italy in their first game of the tournament. Goals from Claudio Marchisio and Mario Balotelli saw Roy Hodgson's side off – who would go home having failed to win a single match at the finals.

ENGLAND'S MOST CAPPED PLAYER, PETER SHILTON, WHO MADE 125 APPEARANCES FOR THE THREE LIONS

JUNE 15

Blackburn Rovers full-back Bob Crompton was celebrating today in 1911 when he became England's most capped player. He was given a portrait of himself after breaking Steve Bloomer's record of 23 England appearances.

The whole nation was celebrating today in 1996 when a Paul Gascoigne inspired England beat Scotland at Wembley. The Euro 96 match was the first meeting between the auld enemies since 1989. Alan Shearer gave England the lead after 53 minutes and Scotland had a chance to equalise on 77 minutes, but David Seaman saved Gary McAllister's penalty. Just a minute later Gazza scored what was later voted the best goal ever scored at Wembley when he lifted the ball over Colin Hendry and then volleyed past Andy Goram in the Scotland goal, celebrating with a re-creation of the 'dentist's chair' routine that had been splashed across the papers in the run-up to the tournament.

JUNE 16

Today in 1982 England were competing in their first World Cup since 1970 and skipper Bryan Robson wasted no time in getting their campaign up and running. Captain Marvel scored after just 27 seconds in the opening match against France as England cantered towards a 3-1 win. It was the fastest goal ever scored in World Cup history and stood for 20 years until Hakan Şükür scored after just ten seconds for Turkey against South Korea in 2002.

Daniel Sturridge's injury time winner nabbed England a Euro 2016 win against Wales on this day – after the Welsh had been 1-0 up at half-time through Gareth Bale. Marcus Rashford also looked lively after coming on as a sub – and thus, at 18 years 228 days, becoming the youngest player to represent England at the Euros.

JUNE 17

There was another iconic image of England failure today in 1992, when Gary Lineker's England career ended with the striker to be forever marooned on 48 international goals, one short of Sir Bobby Charlton's record, after his substitution against Sweden in the European Championships. Graham Taylor's gamble backfired and he was lambasted in the press when England lost the do-or-die game. The *Sun* famously ran the headline 'Swedes 2 Turnips 1', putting a picture of Taylor's head on the aforementioned root vegetable.

After the 1966 World Cup final triumph it took England an incredible 34 years to get another competitive win against their footballing nemesis. It finally happened today at Euro 2000 when an Alan Shearer goal sealed a 1-0 victory. Manager Kevin Keegan said: 'We get fed up in England of people saying Germany have something on us. I would like to think we can make them pay now like they made us pay for 34 years.'

JUNE 18

England had a miserable tournament at Euro 88. Bobby Robson's team's record at the competition in West Germany read: played three, lost three. On this day they played their final match against the USSR before going home, rock bottom of the group with no points. Despite a Tony Adams goal, England lost 3-1.

It was a different story today in 1996 when England dished out an unlikely footballing lesson to Guus Hiddink's Holland at Wembley in their final group match. Alan Shearer and Teddy Sheringham scored two each as the Dutch were dispatched 4-1 by Terry Venables' boys and the nation really started to believe Baddiel and Skinner's contention that football was coming home. Patrick Kluivert scored for Holland late on to ensure they progressed on goal difference at the expense of Scotland.

JUNE 19

Only three sets of fathers and sons have represented England at senior level. Brian and Nigel Clough are among them, Brian having gained two caps in 1959 and Nigel 14, under Bobby Robson and Graham Taylor. Nigel played his last game for England on this day in 1993 in a friendly against Germany in the USA, which England lost 2-1. Neither of them managed to score for England.

England were on the brink of World Cup elimination on this day in 2014 after a Luis Suarez brace gave Uruguay at 2-1 win, just days after England lost to Italy by the same scoreline. It was Suarez's first game back after a month out following knee surgery, and the then-Liverpool striker ruthlessly put England to the sword. The following day Roy Hodgson's side were knocked out when Costa Rica beat Italy.

JUNE 20

Going into the final group match of Euro 2000 against Romania on this day, England needed just a draw to progress to the quarter-final stage. After going a goal down, Alan Shearer and Michael Owen both struck to give England a 2-1 lead at the break. Romania scored again just minutes into the second half but even so Keegan's England looked to have done enough until just two minutes from time when an ugly tackle by Phil Neville gifted a penalty to the opposition. Ioan Ganea scored to send England crashing out of the tournament in Alan Shearer's last game for England. Keegan said: 'If it was about endeavour and honesty we would have won the tournament.'

England did get the result they needed to progress to the next round at the World Cup today in 2006 when two goals from Joe Cole secured a 2-2 draw with Sweden in the final group game. The Three Lions had to continue in the tournament without Michael Owen though, the injury-prone front man crawled off the pitch and out of the World Cup in the first minute of the game with a knee injury.

JUNE 21

Michael Owen gave England a 1-0 lead against Brazil today in 2002 in the World Cup quarter-final to spark hopes of a famous victory over the South Americans. But it was not to be as Rivaldo equalised just before half-time, and Ronaldinho scored the winner after the re-start when he spotted David Seaman off his line and lofted in a free kick from 40 yards out. Ronaldinho was sent off eight minutes later for a foul on Danny Mills but England couldn't make the man advantage tell and were out of yet another World Cup. Captain David Beckham said: 'If anyone makes a scapegoat out of David Seaman after that it will be an absolute disgrace. It was a freak goal.' Gareth Southgate, meanwhile, lamented the lack of an inspirational half-time team-talk from Sven: 'When we needed Winston Churchill, we got Iain Duncan Smith.'

Today at Euro 2004 Wayne Rooney was proving a revelation when he bagged a brace as England beat Croatia 4-2. England boss Sven-Göran Eriksson said: 'I don't remember anyone making such an impact on a tournament since Pelé in the 1958 World Cup.'

JUNE 22

The most infamous match in English football history took place today in the 1986 World Cup quarter-finals in Mexico. Argentine genius Diego Maradona stunned the England players by punching the ball past Peter Shilton to score the most controversial goal in history. With the English still reeling from the Hand of God, Maradona turned on the style for his second goal, dribbling the ball past five defenders before slotting past Shilton for one of the best goals ever seen at the World Cup. Gary Lineker pulled one back for England but the Three Lions were out, and Maradona was unrepentant.

Today at Euro 96 England proved they were in fact capable of winning in a penalty shoot-out. After drawing 0-0 with Spain, England won 4-2 on spot-kicks. Stuart Pearce buried his penalty, and after having missed one in the 1990 World Cup, his reaction is one of the most iconic images of the tournament.

JUNE 23

Preston North End and England defender Bob Holmes was born on this day in 1867 in Preston. As well as playing for his hometown club, Holmes also represented his country and had a great start to his England career – he played in a 5-1 win over Ireland in Belfast in 1888 that meant England won the Home Championship outright for the first time.

A performance that can charitably be described as 'tepid' saw England scrape to a 1-0 World Cup win over Slovenia on this day in 2010. A Jermain Defoe goal gave England the crucial win Fabio Capello's men needed to reach the last 16. Though it was only a temporary reprieve – Germany were waiting for England in their next match…

JUNE 24

Wayne Rooney lit up Euro 2004 with some stunning displays for England. In the quarter-final against Portugal, England were 1-0 up when Rooney had to go off injured and Sven's team immediately lost their spark. After extra time the teams couldn't be separated at 2-2 and the match went to penalties. Captain David Beckham slipped as he skied the first spot kick over the bar. Darius Vassell saw his penalty saved by goalkeeper Ricardo who then stepped up himself to score the winning goal that saw England crash out of yet another tournament on penalties. Michael Owen said: 'It's a big disappointment to lose like this but it always seems to happen. It's a bitter blow.'

Another penalty shootout defeat followed today in 2012, as Ashleys Cole and Young failed to beat Italy 'keeper Gianluigi Buffon from the spot after their Euro 2012 quarter-final ended goalless. It got worse two years to the day later, as a meek 0-0 draw against Costa Rica meant England exited the 2014 World Cup after winning just one point.

JUNE 25

England played their first ever match at a World Cup finals today in 1950 at the Maracanã in Rio de Janeiro. Chile were England's opponents and their team included the inside forward George Robledo who played for Barnsley and Newcastle United. Wilf Mannion and Stan Mortensen bagged the goals for England in a 2-0 win.

At the 2006 World Cup in Germany David Beckham became the first England player to score in three World Cup tournaments on this day. The England captain scored from a free kick in the 1-0 win over Ecuador that secured England's place in the quarter-finals. After an otherwise disappointing match Becks said: 'It was an ugly performance but it was what we wanted and we'll take ugly performances. It was nice to silence a few people who have been critical. I can handle my criticism and I'll prove them wrong. It was a great feeling to get a goal and put us into the quarter-final.'

JUNE 26

England fans dread penalty shoot-outs more than anything so David Platt became a hero on this day at Italia 90 when his goal in the last minute of extra time saw England beat Belgium in their second round tie. With 119 minutes on the clock and the score at 0-0 England won a free kick. Paul Gascoigne floated it in and Platt turned and volleyed home to send England through to the quarter-finals.

England were not so lucky six years later in the semi-final of Euro 96, played on this day. After extra time England and Germany were locked at 1-1 after Alan Shearer's early goal was cancelled out by Stefan Kuntz. In the shoot-out Gareth Southgate's spot kick was saved before Andreas Möller stepped up to score the winner past David Seaman. Southgate should have taken the advice of his mother who later said: 'Why didn't you blast it, dear?' Sadly, England had lost on penalties to Germany, again.

JUNE 27

Kenneth Wolstenholme was immortalised by the words he used to describe the final few moments of the World Cup final in 1966, but he was not the only man commentating on the game for British television. Hugh Johns, who died on this day on 2007, was his opposite number on ITV. While Wolstenholme was uttering his era-defining words, over in the next commentary box at Wembley Johns described the moment with the words: 'Here's Hurst. He might make it three. He has! He has! So that's it!'

There was little for English commentators to get excited about today in 2010, when Fabio Capello's men were dumped out of the World Cup by Germany in controversial fashion. Frank Lampard looked to have crashed in an equaliser off the bar shortly before half-time, only for the officials to wave play on. Ultimately, the Three Lions were outclassed by Joachim Loew's side on their way to a 4-1 defeat.

It got worse still on this day in 2016 when Iceland – a nation of just 330,000 people – sent England packing in the last-16 of Euro 2016. 'That was the worst performance I've ever seen from an England team. Ever,' bemoaned Alan Shearer on the BBC following the 2-1 defeat. Roy Hodgson wasted no time in immediately confirming his resignation following the match as he called time on his four-year Three Lions tenure.

JUNE 28

Graham Poll was the one Englishman who had a realistic hope of being involved in the World Cup final in 2006 but his dream ended on this day when he was sent home from the tournament after a shocking performance in a group game between Australia and Croatia. He managed to show a yellow card to Croatia's Josip Šimunić not once, not twice, but three times before eventually sending him off. Fifa had seen enough and sent him back to Tring with his tail between his legs. Before the tournament began he said prophetically: 'We can't be expected to get everything right.'

JUNE 29

England were on the wrong end of one of the greatest ever upsets today in 1950 at the World Cup in Brazil. As one of the tournament favourites, England were expected to cruise past the part-timers of the USA team – one bookmaker in London was offering 500-1 odds on an American victory. In the match England struggled to break through the USA defence and then five minutes before half-time, Joe Gaetjens scored for the Americans. Despite relentless pressure from England they could not score and the USA team held on to win 1-0. USA defender Harry Keough said: 'Boy, I feel sorry for these bastards. How are they ever going to live down the fact that we beat them?' Back home in England when the result came through to the *Daily Mirror* newsroom a sub-editor assumed it was a mistake and 'corrected' the score to a 10-1 win for England.

Today in 1966 Jimmy Greaves scored four goals in a 6-1 friendly win over Norway. It was his sixth international hat-trick – still an England record. Skipper Bobby Moore also scored that day and it was his second, and last, England goal.

JUNE 30

Today in 1998 saw yet another heroic failure for England, this time at the World Cup in France. Arch rivals Argentina were the opponents in the second round match that saw a penalty for either side converted in the opening ten minutes. Fresh-faced boy wonder Michael Owen then scored the goal of the tournament as he outpaced the Argentine defence and buried the ball past Carlos Roa. Argentina levelled from a free kick and in extra time David Beckham was sent off for his kick at Diego Simeone. Inevitably, England lost the penalty shoot-out and Beckham bore the brunt of the nation's fury.

ENGLAND
ON THIS DAY

JULY

July 1

The Three Lions took on the Indomitable Lions at Italia 90 today, as Cameroon stood between England and the World Cup semi-finals. Led by veteran snake-hipped striker Roger Milla, Cameroon were the tournament's surprise package and took England to the wire, leading 2-1 with ten minutes to go. A brace of Gary Lineker penalties in the 83rd and 105th minutes gave Bobby Robson's men a dramatic extra-time win. 'The country is dancing in the streets now, because we're in the top four in the world in 1990 and I'm proud of that,' said a jubilant Robson.

Another quarter-final in 2006, but with a more depressing ending. England took on Portugal in Gelsenkirchen, and despite losing David Beckham to injury and Wayne Rooney to a red card following Ronaldo's infamous wink, Portugal were held to a 0-0 draw, meaning a penalty shoot-out. Lampard, Carragher and Gerrard all saw their efforts saved by Ricardo and England were out, ending the Sven-Göran Eriksson era.

July 2

'Gareth Southgate, the whole of England is with you… oh it's saved!' The words of Jonathan Pearce as England crashed out of Euro 96 on penalties. Four further penalty shoot-out tournament exits followed for England in the next two decades before, on this day at the 2018 World Cup, the curse was finally lifted when Eric Dier scored the winning spot-kick over Colombia to send the Three Lions through to the quarter-finals. And how fitting that Southgate himself, now England boss, had overseen it. Demons = buried.

In 1950 England's miserable first-ever World Cup experience was finally over as they lost 1-0 to Spain. After their humbling loss to the USA, England started brightly, as Jackie Milburn had a goal incorrectly ruled out for offside, but heroics from Spanish 'keeper Antonio Ramallets ensured a 1-0 Spanish victory. The *Daily Herald* drew up a familiar sounding mock obituary the next day: 'In affectionate remembrance of English football which died in Rio on July 2, 1950… The body will be cremated and the ashes taken to Spain.'

JULY 3

Alf Ramsey's soon-to-be world champions carried on their preparations for the upcoming World Cup today in 1966 with a comfortable 2-0 win over Denmark in Copenhagen. Jack Charlton and George Eastham both netted for the Three Lions, as Jimmy Greaves made his 50th appearance. Chelsea 'keeper Peter Bonetti won the first of his seven England caps, beginning an international career that would end in tears against West Germany in the 1970 World Cup.

After a four-year spell in the footballing wasteland that St James' Park became as the 2000s went on, Michael Owen's career looked dead and buried, with the likes of Hull and Stoke making eyes at the former Liverpool frontman when his Newcastle contract expired. Today in 2009 Fergie shocked the football world by taking a punt on the injury-hit England international, and signed him up on a two-year deal.

JULY 4

The English penalty shoot-out complex was born today in 1990, when England crashed out of Italia 90, losing to West Germany at the semi-final stage. An incident-packed match saw Germany take the lead when Andreas Brehme's shot ballooned over Peter Shilton, via Paul Parker's backside. Gary Lineker's superb equaliser brought about England's third successive extra-time period. In the 99th minute Paul Gascoigne was booked for a mistimed tackle, producing one of English football's most indelible images, as he burst into tears, realising he would be suspended for the final. Yet more drama followed, as Stuart Pearce and Chris Waddle missed their spot kicks to put the German through and ensure that a national obsession with the penalty shoot-out began.

Happier days in 1999 though, if not a tad naff. David Beckham and Spice Girl Victoria Adams were married today at Luttrellstown Castle in Dublin. With Gary Neville as best man, the ceremony featured matching gold thrones for the happy couple, a flock of doves and all manner of cheesiness as the pair set the standard for *OK!* *Magazine* culture and the era of the WAG.

JULY 5

England bowed out of the 1982 World Cup today when they could only draw 0-0 with hosts Spain at the Bernabéu in the final game of the second group phase. Instead of the now-customary loss on penalties England's hard-luck story this time was the fact that they had not lost a single game in the competition, as West Germany – you know they had to be involved – topped the three man group after they had defeated the Spanish three days earlier. This proved to be Ron Greenwood's last match in charge as the man who brought the England team back from the international wilderness of the 1970s retired from the game.

England played their final warm-up match before the 1966 World Cup today, visiting Poland six days before opening the tournament at Wembley. After an epic coach journey from Copenhagen after their last game, Jimmy Greaves stepped off the bus, turned to his manager and said: 'All right, Alf, you've proved your point! Now let's go home!' In front of 93,000 at the Stadion Slaski in Chorzow a full-strength England team recorded a 1-0 win when Roger Hunt struck after 14 minutes as England entered the World Cup on a seven-match winning streak.

JULY 6

Today in 2007, 12 months after leaving the England job, Sven took up the vacant job at Manchester City (having been paid to do nothing by the FA for a year). Putting controversial chairman Thaksin Shinawatra's money to good use he secured a Uefa Cup spot in his first season at Eastlands, but was given the sack soon after, after a period of internal wrangling at the club. Another huge pay-off softened the blow though and a day later he would be appointed Mexico manager.

England again lost to old rivals Germany today in 2000, but this time the action was not on the pitch. After three years of campaigning Germany were awarded the 2006 World Cup, defeating England, South Africa and Morocco in the final voting. England's chances had suffered an insurmountable blow in the days before the vote, as 820 fans were arrested for rioting at the European Championships in Belgium.

JULY 7

England took on host nation Italy in that curious beast, the World Cup third-fourth place match today in 1990. Roberto Baggio and Golden Boot winner Salvatore Schillaci sandwiched an effort from David Platt, one of the English revelations of the tournament, to give the Azzurri a 2-1 win. England fans were saying farewell to manager Bobby Robson – eight years to the day since he replaced Ron Greenwood – and also 'keeper Peter Shilton who ended his 20-year international career on 125 caps, which remains the England record.

The Three Lions matched their Italia 90 last-four exploits 28 years later, sweeping aside Sweden 2-0 in the quarter-finals of the World Cup today in 2018. Harry Maguire's set-piece opener and a Dele Alli second-half strike were enough to keep the Swedes at arm's length and set up a semi-final against Croatia.

JULY 8

Former England boss Terry Venables landed the manager's job at Leeds United today in 2002. Since leaving the Three Lions after Euro 96 El Tel had spells with Australia and Crystal Palace before acting as Bryan Robson's managerial pair of stabilisers at Middlesbrough. He failed to see the season out at Elland Road after being forced to sell England defenders Rio Ferdinand and Jonathan Woodgate as a result of the Yorkshire side's well-documented financial problems.

Conservative Party leader William Hague used football for some political point-scoring today in 1999 when he attacked Tony Blair over Manchester United's decision to pull out of the FA Cup to compete in the World Club Championship to help England's bid to host the 2006 World Cup. Hague said the move had 'this government's fingerprints all over it', and Alex Ferguson claimed 'we have been under considerable pressure from the government', but Blair and sports minister Tony Banks denied putting the squeeze on United.

JULY 9

Jamie Carragher isn't one to take criticism lying down. After growing frustrated with empty promises from Steve McClaren over his place in the England team, Carragher announced he was quitting the international game, a decision that rankled *TalkSPORT* host Adrian Durham. Within minutes the Liverpool defender was on the phone: 'Don't you ever call me a bottler on radio,' he fired in his scouse drawl. 'It would be interesting to see if you've got any bottle if you come down here and say it to me at Anfield or Melwood on a Champions League night.'

Lightning Seeds frontman Ian Broudie, the man behind England's anthemic 'Three Lions' song from Euro 96 announced today in 1998 that it was unlikely he would ever play the song again. Glenn Hoddle's men were days away from crashing out of France 98 when the Lightning Seeds played the song for the last time at the Glastonbury festival. A downbeat Broudie said: 'At Glastonbury everyone was going for it in the rain and it was a really great moment, but it's time to move on creatively now.'

JULY 10

Two of England's Italia 90 alumni were on the move today in 1995. David Platt, whose memorable strike against Belgium was referenced in 'Three Lions', had enjoyed his Italian experience so much he became somewhat of a Serie A journeyman, turning out for Bari, Juventus and Sampdoria. Today he moved back to his homeland, signing for Arsenal in a £4.75m move. Following him back to the UK was Paul Gascoigne who called time on his turbulent three-year Lazio career to join Rangers for a fee of £4.3m.

Going the other way on that same day was Paul Ince, who left Manchester United for Internazionale in a £7.5m deal. Ince's relations with Alex Ferguson were frosty at the best of times, with the Scot labelling the England captain a 'big-time Charlie' and accusing him of engineering the move to Serie A. After two impressive, but trophy-less years at the San Siro Ince returned to the Premiership, joining Liverpool.

JULY 11

The 1966 World Cup began today when England took on Uruguay, with few signs that this would be England's year. The Three Lions failed to score at Wembley for the first time in 52 post-war games, as they were held to a 0-0 draw. Alf Ramsey was feeling the pressure, refusing to do a post-match interview with the BBC, saying: 'I was available before and no-one wanted me. Now it's too late.' Former Scotland international Billy Liddell offered a pessimistic view of their chances: 'Let's not talk too much about England winning the World Cup,' he said. 'We ought to be more worried about whether they are going to qualify from the group.'

England came up agonisingly short in their first World Cup semi-final since Italia 90 today in 2018. Croatia striker Mario Mandzukic scored an extra-time winner against Gareth Southgate's side to dash English hopes of ending 52 years of hurt.

JULY 12

After their underwhelming performance the day before, Alf Ramsey took his 1966 World Cup squad on a morale-boosting visit to the set of the new James Bond film, *You Only Live Twice*. With the booze flowing, the team were given an inspirational speech from Bond himself, Sean Connery, who, legend has it, almost signed for Manchester United as a youngster. Showing his usual way with words Ramsey said: 'Thank you Seen,' to which Jimmy Greaves turned to his pal Bobby Moore and quipped: 'That's the funniest thing I've ever shorn.'

Ramsey's England predecessor Don Revie was having a rather less enjoyable day today in 1977, as the *Daily Mail* revealed he was ditching England for a lucrative job coaching the United Arab Emirates. With England struggling to qualify for the 1978 World Cup, and convinced he was about to be sacked, Revie made a clandestine visit to the Middle East, dressed in dark glasses and bulky overcoat. He agreed a £60,000-a-year tax-free deal with a £100,000 bonus; the nation quickly turned on him; the FA attempted to ban him from football for 10 years for bringing the game into disrepute. They failed, but Revie's reputation never recovered.

July 13

Former England captain David Platt was given the job of England under-21 manager today in 2001. Platt gave up his role as Nottingham Forest manager to fill the post, where he had heavily spent on new players, but with little success. He fared slightly better as the under-21 boss, taking his side to the European Championships in 2002, although they would finish bottom of their group and then fail to qualify for the 2004 competition.

One of Platt's England teammates, Steve Bull, announced his retirement today in 1999. Despite playing for Second Division Wolves, Bull played 13 times for England between 1989 and 1990, scoring four goals and been part of the World Cup 1990 squad before being overlooked by Graham Taylor.

July 14

The FA announced today in 1997 that they would close their School of Excellence at Lilleshall. The centre had been set up in 1984 and was modelled on the successful French academy at Clairefontaine, but was closed after criticism of its centralist and perceived anti-club agenda. Over its 15 years 234 players went through the system, including Andy Cole, Sol Campbell, Michael Owen, Joe Cole and Jermain Defoe, but FA technical director Howard Wilkinson scrapped the school in favour of club academies and centres of excellence.

England may have ultimately come up short at the 2018 World Cup, but skipper Harry Kane did go home with some silverware – his six goals winning him the Golden Boot. It was on this day that England lost their third-place play-off match 2-0 to Belgium. Kane didn't score, but neither did his closest rival for the award, Romelu Lukaku. Kane's win was secured after the following day's final when no other player managed to surpass his total.

A BLOODIED TERRY BUTCHER LEADS ENGLAND TO WORLD CUP QUALIFICATION AGAINST SWEDEN IN 1989

JULY 15

The English transfer record was shattered today in 1994 when Blackburn Rovers paid Norwich City £5m for striker Chris Sutton. In his first season at Ewood Park he slotted in alongside Alan Shearer, developing a formidable partnership that they looked set to replicate on the international stage. However, injuries and a row with Glenn Hoddle over Sutton's refusal to play in the England B team meant that he made one appearance for the Three Lions, when he came on as a substitute in a friendly against Cameroon in November 1997.

A freshly-minted Chelsea splashed out on Southampton's England left-back Wayne Bridge today in 2003, spending £8m of new owner Roman Abramovich's hard-earned cash, with Bridge's predecessor in the England defence Graeme le Saux moving in the opposite direction.

JULY 16

England bounced back from their disappointing opening World Cup game today in 1966 by downing Mexico 2-0, although England again flattered to deceive. After 30 goalless minutes a restless 92,570-strong Wembley crowd began to sing 'we want goals!' and it was up to Bobby Charlton to oblige with a 37th minute piledriver. The younger Charlton brother turned provider in the second half, teeing up Jimmy Greaves, whose shot was parried by the Mexican keeper, but only as far as Roger Hunt who slotted home. England were up and running.

Today in 2006 former England boss Terry Venables announced that he was in talks with new national team manager Steve McClaren about a return to the England set-up. After signing on, he spent 18 games sat next to McClaren on the England bench, donning a snazzy waistcoat for the pair's first game against Greece, but was sacked after the Croatia debacle in November 2007.

JULY 17

Kenneth Wolstenholme, the man who coined the most famous phrase in England football history was born today in 1920. During the 1950s and '60s Wolstenholme was the BBC's go-to guy, covering every major game including the Three Lions' most famous day in 1966, where he came up with the ditty that has loomed large over the nation's collective imagination ever since: 'And here comes Hurst, he's got... some people are on the pitch, they think it's all over! ... It is now!' He only received £60 for his work in the Wembley commentary box that day and was ousted by the Beeb four years later to make way for David Coleman.

Wolstenholme ended his career commentating on Paul Gascoigne in Serie A and Gazza was on the move today in 2000 leaving Middlesbrough to join up with his former Rangers boss Walter Smith at Everton on a free transfer. He immediately targeted a return to the England squad, saying: 'I've already got my eye on an Everton season ticket for Kevin Keegan.' The call never came though, as persistent injury and fitness doubts plagued his two-year spell at Goodison and limited him to only 32 appearances for the Toffeemen.

JULY 18

A young Robbie Fowler was making a name for himself today in 1993, as England under-18 defeated France in the European Championships at the Victoria Ground in Stoke. The Liverpool frontman came off the bench to score from 25 yards after fellow substitute Kevin Gallen had given England the lead. Also featuring in the Three Lions' 2-0 win were Gary Neville, Sol Campbell, Nicky Butt and Paul Scholes in front of a crowd of 6,756.

Nick Barmby scored the first England goals of both the Glenn Hoddle and Sven-Göran Eriksson regimes and today in 2000 the midfielder did the unthinkable and crossed Stanley Park to join Liverpool from their bitter rivals Everton in a £6m move.

JULY 19

Stuart Pearce signed on to become the full-time England under-21 coach today in 2007, a month after had overseen a heart-breaking 13-12 penalty shoot-out loss to the Netherlands in the European under-21 Championships semi-finals as part-time manager. Pearce's impressive young charges went one step further in the 2009 edition, but suffered a crushing 4-0 defeat to their manager's old nemesis Germany in the final.

Former England captain Stanley Harris was born today in 1881. Harris skippered the England side on four occasions in the 1900s and the Old Westminsters FC inside-left also found time to carve out a decent county cricket career, representing Cambridge University, Gloucestershire, Surrey and Sussex.

JULY 20

England's 1966 campaign stepped up a gear today when they beat France to win group one and secure their place in the quarter-finals. As in their previous two games, England made heavy weather of their opponents, despite two key French players, Robert Herbin and Jacky Simon, sustaining injuries during the game, in this, the age before substitutes. Nobby Stiles was booked for his wild challenge on Simon and after the match Fifa and FA bosses called to have Stiles banned from the tournament. Ramsey met up with his masters at the FA and proclaimed, 'If he goes, so do I. You will be looking for a few manager.' Two Roger Hunt goals were enough for England to win 2-0 in Jimmy Greaves' final match of the tournament, after the Tottenham striker was kicked in the shin by Joseph Bonnel and needed four stitches. Some bloke named Hurst then came in to take his place in the team.

In 2004, with England's hope of silverware that summer long gone, manager Sven-Göran Eriksson turned his attention away from football to his other passion: womanising. Today it emerged that Svennis had been playing away from home and having an affair with FA secretary Faria Alam. Sven rode out the media storm, as kiss-and-tell tabloid interviews and a spell on *Celebrity Big Brother* followed for Faria.

JULY 21

England took on Switzerland today in 1945 to celebrate the 50th anniversary of the Swiss FA. As was the case with all internationals during and immediately after the Second World War, this was not recognised as an official match and this was just as well for England, as a side featuring the likes of Tom Finney, Tommy Lawton and Joe Mercer went down 3-1 in Berne. Robert Brown of Charlton Athletic scored England's consolation goal.

David Beckham made his LA Galaxy debut today in 2007 when he came on as a substitute against Chelsea in the somewhat over-the-top named World Series of Soccer. Coming on after 78 minutes, Beckham made his bow on US soil in front of a capacity crowd of 27,000 at the Home Depot Center, but couldn't stop a 1-0 Chelsea win thanks to a goal from John Terry, the man that replaced LA's marquee signing as England skipper.

JULY 22

Combine Rio Ferdinand's superb performances in the 2002 World Cup finals with Leeds United's perilous financial position at the time and a big money move away from Elland Road was inevitable. Manchester United raided their cross-Pennine rivals for the former West Ham centre-back today in 2002, shelling out a British record £30m in the process.

Two years later an opportunistic Spaniard put the ball that David Beckham had blasted over the bar during the Euro 2004 quarter-final penalty shoot-out up for sale on eBay. The fan ended up making over £6,000 due to Beckham's hapless effort against Portugal, so at least someone other than the Germans and Portuguese has benefited from England's inability to score from 12 yards.

JULY 23

England's World Cup challenge reached the quarter-final stage today in 1966 as they took on Argentina in one of the most fiery matches in the tournament's history. The South Americans had already picked up a warning from Fifa over their conduct during their group game with West Germany and got stuck into England right from the first whistle. Shortly before half-time the argumentative Argentine captain Antonio Rattin was red carded 'for the look on his face', according to the referee and would refuse to leave the pitch for ten minutes, sitting on the Queen's red carpet and spouting out all manner of conspiracy theories that the game was fixed. England eventually won the bad-tempered clash 1-0 thanks to a late Geoff Hurst header.

After the game Alf Ramsey stormed onto the pitch to stop his players swapping shirts with the Argentineans, who responded by trying to break into the England dressing room. Ramsey's un-diplomatic post-game comments saw him forever endear himself and the England team to Argentina when he said: 'Our best football will come against the team which comes out to play football, and not to act as animals.'

JULY 24

Today in 1945 England continued their mini-tour of Switzerland by facing off against a Swiss B team in Zurich. Goals from Tom Finney, Willie Watson and Michael Fenton gave the Three Lions a 3-0 win in this unofficial match, that was originally classed as a Services XI side, but that was later changed to an England XI when the FA wrote their official history in 1953.

David Beckham was in the headlines again today in 2003 when he arrived for his first day at Real Madrid following his £25m move. A gaggle of press and fans were at the Madrid training ground to meet the newest Galáctico as the club prepared for a money-spinning tour of Asia to show off their newest asset.

July 25

England's on-off flirtation with Fifa ended today in 1946 when the FA finally returned to the international fold. After originally joining in 1906 they left in 1928 over an argument on amateur payments. Realising the rest of the world were happy to move on in their absence England agreed to sign up, with the rest of the British associations following. A friendly match between Great Britain and a Rest of Europe XI raised £35,000 for Fifa, which was struggling financially after the war. Four years later England even entered their first World Cup, but after the infamous 1-0 loss to the USA they probably wish they hadn't.

The England under-18 team were crowned European Champions today in 1993 when they defeated Turkey 1-0 in the final at the City Ground. Tottenham's Darren Caskey was the hero, netting a penalty 13 minutes from time to win the title for the ninth time and first since 1980.

July 26

The Three Lions roared into the World Cup final today in 1966, defeating a Eusébio-inspired Portugal side 2-1. The game was originally meant to be played at Anfield, but FA officials controversially saw that the clash was moved to Wembley. Both sides had come off the back of draining quarter-final wins, with England being kicked off the park by Argentina and Portugal coming back from 3-0 down to defeat North Korea 5-3, but they contrived to put on one of the most entertaining matches of the competition.

An attacking display from both sides saw England take a first-half lead through Bobby Charlton, as Nobby Stiles put the shackles on Eusébio. Before the game Alf Ramsey had told the Manchester United enforcer to take the Portuguese playmaker out, to which he replied: 'For one game or a whole career?' Bobby Charlton added a second goal with ten minutes remaining and England would hold on, despite a late Eusébio penalty after Jack Charlton handled on the line, and reach their first World Cup final.

JULY 27

Recent years have seen a rash of teenagers in the England team, with the likes of Theo Walcott and Wayne Rooney paving the way for Gareth Southgate's trust in youth, but this faith in youngsters is a relatively new thing. Before Wayne Rooney came along in 2003 the record for England's youngest ever player was held for 124 years by Clapham Rovers half-back James Prinsep who was born today in 1861. Prinsep also held the record for the youngest player in an FA Cup Final for 125 years but this record was broken a year after his England landmark was bettered by Millwall's Curtis Weston.

Alan Shearer broke the British transfer record for the first time today in 1992 when Blackburn Rovers, freshly minted thanks to Jack Walker, splashed out £3.6m for the young Southampton striker who had made a goalscoring debut for the Three Lions earlier that year. Shearer would pick up the only major honour of his career at Ewood Park, when Rovers won the 1994/95 Premiership title.

JULY 28

Wolves legend Ron Flowers, the oldest member of the 1966 World Cup squad, was born today in 1934. Flowers was agonisingly close to playing in the World Cup final, as Jack Charlton was suffering from a cold on the eve of England's biggest ever match, causing Alf Ramsey to put Flowers on standby. After a sleepless night for Flowers, Charlton awoke feeling fine and took to the field. Flowers ended his England career after the tournament on 49 caps and was one of the '66 squad members that received their winner's medals in 2009.

Also celebrating his birthday today is Ray Kennedy, one of England's most decorated players. During spells with Arsenal and Liverpool, Kennedy, who was born in 1951, won every domestic honour going, picking up 17 England caps in the process.

JULY 29

Following his Golden Boot antics earlier that summer in Euro 96 Alan Shearer became the world's most expensive player today when fellow Geordie messiah Kevin Keegan paid Blackburn £15m to bring the striker back home to Newcastle. Shearer toiled away at St James' for ten years, becoming the Toon's record goalscorer, but didn't achieve much else of note until returning to manage and ultimately relegate the club in 2009.

Paul Gascoigne made a typically rambunctious debut for Rangers today in 1995 in the Ibrox International Tournament against Steaua Bucharest. Sporting a short bleach-blonde haircut, Gazza showed both sides of his game in the five minutes before half-time, almost being sent off after lashing out at Steaua's Damian Militaru before scoring his first goal for the Gers seconds later.

JULY 30

At 5.15 in the afternoon today in 1966, the final whistle blew at Wembley Stadium, seconds after Geoff Hurst had completed his hat-trick and Kenneth Wolstenholme had uttered those immortal words. England had done it and were World Champions for the first and, so far, only time in their history after beating West Germany 4-2. Alf Ramsey had guaranteed an English victory at a press conference the day before and the final itself had everything: two fierce rivals, goals galore, controversy, extra time, a pitch invasion and, for once, a happy ending for the Three Lions. Goals from Geoff Hurst and Martin Peters had put England seconds away from victory, but a last-gasp equaliser from Wolfgang Weber forced the game into extra time. Ramsey then rallied his troops by pointing to the Germans and saying: 'Look at them! They're finished! You've won it once, now you'll have to go out there and win it again.' And this is exactly what they did, as Hurst's controversial second goal was awarded by the so-called Russian linesman, who actually came from Azerbaijan, before scoring a famous third. Cue Mr Wolstenholme: 'There's some people on the pitch, they think it's all over... It is now!'

JULY 31

Tributes were paid today in 2009 when Sir Bobby Robson lost his long battle against cancer. As a player, he won 20 England caps whilst at West Brom, returning to the national side as manager in 1982 for an eight-year spell in charge. At Italia 90 Robson silenced the critics that had maligned him in the run-up to the tournament, taking England to within a penalty shoot-out of the World Cup final, as a new era dawned on English football. Sir Bobby then left the England job to manage PSV, Sporting Lisbon, Porto and Barcelona before returning to his native north-east to take over at Newcastle with a clutch of honours. His death was met by a huge outpouring of grief from all corners of the footballing world, as the game lost one of its most respected, passionate and loved individuals.

Today in 1998 Liverpool announced that they wanted to insure their boy wonder Michael Owen for £60m over the next six years of his contract against injury, accident or illness. Showing remarkable insight, several insurance companies were frightened off by Liverpool's valuation despite a six-figure premium, knowing a bad deal when they saw it. At the time £60m could have bought you 857 12kg gold bars, half a jumbo jet or 387 Rolls Royces and lord knows how many career-salvaging glossy promotional brochures.

Leeds United striker Allan 'Sniffer' Clarke was born today in 1946. Clarke scored ten goals in his 19 England appearances, including a high-pressure penalty on his debut against Czechoslovakia in a 1-0 win in England's first 1970 World Cup match. He also dispatched a spot-kick in England's infamous 1-1 draw with Poland in 1973 that cost the Three Lions a place in the 1974 World Cup and ultimately lead to Sir Alf Ramsey losing his job.

ENGLAND
ON THIS DAY

AUGUST

AUGUST 1

He may seem about as sexually alluring as a bowl of cold soup but Sven-Göran Eriksson must have had something behind those rimless glasses as his womanising exploits are legion. Today in 2004 further details emerged following Sven's latest conquest, FA secretary Faria Alam. The *News of the World* reported that not only had Ms Alam succumbed to the Swede's charms, but had also slept with his boss, FA chief executive Mark Palios, in the most bizarre love triangle this side of the New Order song. The FA initially tried to deny the whole thing. 'When it first broke we thought it was a reasonable story because it was the England boss having an affair. What we did not expect was that it would run for four weeks in a row on the front page,' Gary Thompson, associate editor of the *News of the World* told the *Guardian*. 'The reason it stayed there was because the FA's immediate response to the story was to deny it through their lawyers. We got heavy legal letters denying it after the first allegations, and we knew it was true.'

AUGUST 2

Combative England midfielder Dennis 'the menace' Wise was living up to his troublesome reputation today in 2002 when his club Leicester City sacked him after he punched teammate Callum Davidson in the face, breaking his cheekbone. Bobby Gould who managed Wise at Wimbledon said: 'He made himself into a top-class player – he was always looking for the ball but there was that edge, and unfortunately that's what has cost him.'

England captain David Beckham made his debut for new club Real Madrid today in 2003 after his much-hyped £25m move from Manchester United. Becks started his first match in the famous white shirt in a friendly in Beijing against the scary-sounding China Dragons. He played on the right of a Galáctico-studded midfield and displayed some typically good passing and threatened the Dragons' goal with a couple of trademark free kicks but failed to score as Real won 4-0.

AUGUST 3

Paul Scholes, the midfield ginger genius, announced his retirement from international football on this day in 2004, after England had bowed out of Euro 2004 at their customary quarter-final point. The Manchester United star who played 66 times for England and scored 14 goals said: 'I started my England career in 1997 and have enjoyed seven years of great football, playing in the best competitions, with some of the best players, under the best managers. Euro 2004 was fantastic but afterwards I felt the time was right for myself and my family to make it my last England appearance.' Sven-Göran Eriksson said: 'Paul and I have been speaking about this since Euro 2004. While he remained a key part of my plans for the England team, I fully respect his decision. He has a very special talent and it has been a privilege working so closely with him.'

AUGUST 4

England utility man Phil Neville was on the move today in 2005 when he left Manchester United and joined Everton for £3m. Younger brother of Gary, Phil's versatility was his downfall at club and country level, as he struggled to make any one position his own. Finally fed up at playing second fiddle to just about every other player in the United squad, Phil decided to leave so he could play every week. Alex Ferguson said: 'This was not a decision we wanted to make, but every time I picked the team and Phil's name was not on the team sheet, it was very difficult for me.' Neville told the Manchester United website: 'This has been the most difficult decision I have ever had to make.'

Britain declared war on Germany today in 1914 and although domestic matches in England carried on through the 1914-15 season, the international game was suspended. More than five years had passed since the Three Lions' last game when they made the trip to Belfast in October 1919 and played out a 1-1 draw with Ireland at Windsor Park.

AUGUST 5

If there is one thing England fans dread at every major tournament, it is a penalty shoot-out. England have exited three World Cups and three European Championships thanks to profligacy from the spot, losing out to Germany and Portugal (both twice), Argentina and Italy. Today in 1970 the cruellest of ways to decide a game was first used in an English football match. Hull City were the unfortunate team to fall foul of the shoot-out, in a match against Manchester United in the long-forgotten Watney Mann Invitation Cup. After drawing their match at Boothferry Park United came out on top in the shoot-out. The same year Fifa and Uefa adopted the method for their competitions and England have toiled ever since.

The first ever match at the new Wembley Stadium was not in fact the friendly against Brazil, but a charity match between former professionals and a celebrity team in aid of former England player Geoff Thomas's foundation. After he retired Thomas – who was born today in 1964 – was diagnosed with leukaemia. He has now recovered and spends his time raising money for his charity.

AUGUST 6

The one bright spot for England at the 2006 World Cup in Germany was Joe Cole. The midfielder was England's best player at the tournament, weighed in with some crucial goals and looked to have finally solved England's long-standing left-sided problem. Today in 2003 Cole left his boyhood club West Ham and signed for London rivals Chelsea for £6.6m. As a Hammer, he had been captain when the club were relegated from the Premiership and when Roman Abramovich's riches came-a-calling Joey couldn't resist. 'It's been a difficult decision but I feel it is time to leave West Ham,' he said. His move took Chelsea's spending that summer to £58m.

One of the players in the first World Cup England bothered with was born today in 1925. Tottenham player Eddie Baily won the first of his nine caps in a match against Spain in the 1950 World Cup in Brazil.

AUGUST 7

England captain Alan Shearer was not leading by example today in 1999 when he was sent off for the first time in his career while on duty for Newcastle. The Geordie number nine was shown the red card by Uriah Rennie at St James' Park for a second-half foul on Aston Villa's Ian Taylor.

Rather peculiarly, Rupert Sandilands earned all but one of his five England caps playing against Wales. The Old Westminsters player was born today in 1868 and is in that exclusive club of international players to score on their debut, against Wales in 1892.

AUGUST 8

Can you remember who played in the left midfield position for England in the 5-1 defeat of Germany in Munich in 2001? Nicky Barmby was the man who was the latest to be tried in England's long-time troubled position. On this day in 2002 Terry Venables, Barmby's ex-manager at Tottenham and with England, tried to turn back the clock and signed him for Leeds United from Liverpool for £2.75m. Barmby, who won 23 caps and scored four goals for England, was El Tel's first signing as manager of the Yorkshire club.

Despite scoring 18 goals when often starting games from the bench, Michael Owen's days at Real Madrid were clearly numbered after just one season at the Bernabéu when they signed Robinho and Júlio Baptista. While Owen would have preferred to return to Liverpool Rafa Benítez didn't seem all that keen to have him back. Newcastle were keen though and today in 2005 former chairman Freddy Shepherd contacted Madrid to get the ball rolling on the most disastrous career move Owen would ever make.

AUGUST 9

When Sir Alf Ramsey was sacked as England manager in 1974, the FA turned to former Manchester City boss Joe Mercer to lead the team until a permanent appointment was made. Mercer was in charge for seven matches, winning three, drawing three and losing one during which time England won the Home Championship (jointly with Scotland). He died of a stroke on this day in 1990, his 76th birthday.

Goodness knows what Sir Alf would have made of events in Los Angeles today when former England skipper David Beckham made his MLS debut for LA Galaxy. Despite the mass hysteria in the stands – one fan screamed 'He's literally warming up now!' into a mobile phone totally ignoring the actual game being played on the pitch – Becks' contribution was fairly minimal and the Galaxy were beaten 1-0 by DC United.

AUGUST 10

Not many players score on their debut for England, but it was lucky for Francis Jeffers that he did against Australia in 2003, as he will likely never get another chance to net for his country. Today in 2004 Arsene Wenger finally admitted his mistake and sold his 'fox in the box' to Charlton for £2.6m.

Chelsea defender John Terry was named the new captain of England by Steve McClaren today in 2006, after David Beckham had resigned the post following the 2006 World Cup. McClaren said: 'John has all the attributes an international captain needs – leadership, authority, courage, ability, tactical awareness and a total refusal to accept second-best. He has been an inspiration for Chelsea and is at his best in adversity.' JT added: 'It is the ultimate honour to be the captain of your country and I am very proud to be given this great opportunity. It is an incredible challenge and one I am looking forward to very much.'

AUGUST 11

When he was given the job as England boss Steve McClaren tried early on to assert his authority on the team. Today in 2006 he announced his first squad for a friendly against Greece, and omitted David Beckham. 'I told David I was looking to change things, looking to go in a different direction, and he wasn't included within that,' explained McClaren. Beckham said: 'I'm proud to have played for England for ten years and my passion for representing my country remains as strong as ever.' After a few shaky England performances McClaren swallowed his pride and recalled Becks for the prestige friendly against Brazil.

The very same day McClaren was dispensing with one of the old guard, he also decided to take on one of his predecessors as his assistant. Former England boss Terry Venables was named as McClaren's assistant today in 2006. 'I feel wonderful to be involved again,' said Venables. 'It is a great privilege.' His appointment immediately sparked suggestions he could usurp McClaren if things went badly but he insisted: 'I am not looking to be a rival. I am looking to help Steve. We will get the balance right.'

AUGUST 12

Former England midfielder David Rocastle was on the move today in 1994 when he was sold by Manchester City to Chelsea for £1.25m. 'The move came completely out of the blue,' Rocastle said. 'I was on my way to training this morning and was told that the club had accepted a good offer from Chelsea. Chelsea are a young side with a lot of good players. Following their success last year they're in Europe. Hopefully I can use my experience to help them and I'm looking forward to some exciting times.' Sadly he died in 2001 of cancer, aged just 33.

Glenn Hoddle was making backroom changes to the England set-up today in 1996 when he decided not to renew the contract of long-time England coach Don Howe. Meanwhile Hoddle persuaded left-back Stuart Pearce to come out of international retirement. 'I'm thrilled Stuart has changed his mind,' said Hoddle.

AUGUST 13

England striker Michael Owen was once as synonymous with Liverpool as Steven Gerrard but today in 2004, after becoming frustrated at the club's lack of progress in the Premiership and the Champions League, he left for Real Madrid. Liverpool won the Champions League in their first season without him. At Madrid, Owen won nothing.

After being sacked by England, Steve McClaren went off to Holland to try and restore his reputation. The first competitive match with his new side FC Twente, was a Champions League qualifier against Arsenal on this day in 2008. His side lost 2-0 but in the build up to the game he was filmed giving an interview to Dutch television speaking in a bizarre Dutch accent. The wally with the brolly said: 'Championsh League, Liverpool or Arshenal, I thought one of them we would draw and it is Arshenal I think. To experiensh big gamesh, Championsh League... Arshenal... The Emiratesh... will be fantashtic for the playersh, not just for now but for the future ash well. I shay I think we are not just... what you call?... underdogsh but mashive underdogsh.'

AUGUST 14

The fall-out from England's 1998 World Cup exit continued today when the *Sun* newspaper printed the first extract from Glenn Hoddle's *World Cup Diary* book. Among the many revelations from within the England team, the book revealed how Paul Gascoigne acted 'like a man possessed' when he was dropped from the France 98 squad. Hoddle was slammed in the press for publishing the book, and the FA were criticised for not having read the manuscript before allowing its publication. PFA chief Gordon Taylor told the *Daily Express*: 'A manager's relationship with his players should be like a doctor with his patient. Players in the squad will be very wary of Glenn now and I don't think it is going to help his relationship with them. They will be worried that their discussions are going to reappear somewhere down the line. This is not the sort of thing we should expect from the England coach.'

KEVIN KEEGAN HEADS FOR THE WEMELEY TOILETS AFTER ENGLAND LOSE 1-0 TO GERMANY IN THEIR FINAL GAME AT THE OLD WEMBLEY STADIUM IN 2000

AUGUST 15

Sven-Göran Eriksson tasted defeat as England boss for the first time today in 2001 when his team were outclassed by Holland in a friendly at White Hart Lane. Eriksson displayed his penchant for mass substitutions by making 11 changes during the game, including twice replacing the goalkeeper. Only a bemused Jamie Carragher played the full 90 minutes of the 2-0 defeat. Owen Hargreaves made his England debut and became only the second player, after Joe Baker in 1959, to play for England without ever having played club football in England.

Another young player due to make his England debut was Dean Ashton, who was included in Steve McClaren's first squad for a friendly against Greece. Sadly for Ashton, he broke his ankle in training today in 2006 and was ruled out for a whole year. He finally made his international debut two years later under Fabio Capello.

AUGUST 16

England played Greece at Old Trafford today in 2006 with Steve McClaren taking charge for the very first time. As unbelievable as it sounds now, the former Middlesbrough boss was hailed as a genius after a superb display say England thrash the European Champions 4-0. Having dropped David Beckham, McClaren put Steven Gerrard on the right wing, had Owen Hargreaves anchoring the midfield, allowed Lampard a free attacking role, and played Stewart Downing on the left. He seemed to have finally solved the conundrum of getting Lampard and Gerrard to play together and the fans were even chanting the new boss's name. As false dawns go, it was a belter.

In the same match Chris Kirkland made his long-awaited England debut, coming on for Paul Robinson at half-time. His appearance made his dad and a group of friends £10,000 each – they had all placed £100 bets at 100/1 in 1992 that the then schoolboy would one day represent his country.

AUGUST 17

As one of the youngsters emerging from the academy into the Manchester United first team, David Beckham was already making a name for himself in the mid-nineties, but today in 1996, on the first day of the new Premiership season, Becks made himself a household name when he scored from the halfway line against Wimbledon after noticing keeper Neil Sullivan was off his line. He was brought into the England squad soon after.

England suffered their worst defeat for 25 years today in 2005 in a friendly match away to Denmark designed to allow the team to prepare for some crucial upcoming qualification matches for the 2006 World Cup. After a goalless first half, England conceded three goals in seven minutes in a 4-1 defeat. David James came on for the second half and had to pick the ball out of the net four times. He later blamed his lack of preparation for his poor performance. He said: 'Because I knew I wasn't going to start I did not do my starting preparations – but you should always prepare to play. I did not adhere to that and everyone saw the results.'

AUGUST 18

Shaun Wright-Phillips made his England debut and the headlines on this day in 2004. The diminutive Manchester City winger came on in the second half of a friendly against Ukraine played at Newcastle's St James' Park. England were already leading 2-0 through goals from stalwarts David Beckham and Michael Owen, but SWP added the third in a 3-0 win on 72 minutes when he ran with the ball from his own half before pulling a right-footed shot across Alexander Shovkovsky to score a trademark goal.

Kieron Dyer continued his stuttering England career when he was sent on by Eriksson at half-time. As a Newcastle player it would normally have been a privilege to play for England on his home ground, but after a recent bust up with manager Sir Bobby Robson his appearance was roundly booed by the fans.

AUGUST 19

When Fabio Capello took over as England boss he was rather bemused about how much importance the English place on who is the captain, saying that in Italy, it is simply the player with the most experience. After trying out several different players in the role in his first few games including Steven Gerrard, Rio Ferdinand and David Beckham, it was John Terry who, today in 2008, got the nod from the Italian to continue in the role Steve McClaren had given him in 2006. Terry said Rio, who was tipped for the job, took the news well. 'The first thing Rio did was turn to me and shake my hand, and that's a measure of the kind of guy he is,' JT said.

On the very same day, England's under-21 team were showing their determination when they battled back from being a goal down to Slovenia to win a friendly 2-1 thanks to goals from James Milner and Micah Richards at the KC Stadium in Hull.

AUGUST 20

For most of Sven-Göran Eriksson's reign as England boss Michael Owen and David Beckham provided most of the goals and so it was again today in 2003 when a goal each helped England defeat Croatia 3-1 in a friendly match at Ipswich's Portman Road. The third England goal came from Chelsea midfielder Frank Lampard – it was his first goal for his country.

Neither Owen nor Beckham was playing for England in another friendly against the Czech Republic at Wembley today in 2008. It was Fabio Capello's fifth match in charge of the team and probably his most disappointing as England were outplayed by the visitors who twice led the game only to be pegged back both times. Wes Brown scored his first goal for England and Joe Cole spared Capello's blushes with an equaliser as the referee was about to blow for full time.

AUGUST 21

England captain Alan Shearer got over the disappointment of losing the Euro 96 semi-final by becoming Kevin Keegan's flagship £15m signing at hometown club Newcastle. The number nine made his Magpies debut against Wimbledon today in 1996 at St James' Park. England colleague David Batty scored the opener but Shearer managed to steal the limelight with just two minutes to go when he delighted the fans by netting on his first outing in the black and white shirt.

And now to a player who has an even better goals-per-game ratio in an England shirt than Alan Shearer. Former Everton, Nottingham Forest and Derby striker Frank Wignall played only twice for England, against Wales and Holland in 1964. He scored twice on his debut against Wales.

AUGUST 22

John Brockbank was born on this day in 1848. Twenty-four years later he was one of 22 men who made history when he took to the field as one of the England players in the first ever international match against Scotland. He never played for his country again.

Germany defeated England in the last ever match played in the old Wembley Stadium. How fitting then, that they should also be the first team to beat England in the new stadium seven years later, on this day in 2007. Frank Lampard gave Steve McClaren's side an early lead but Kevin Kuranyi and a thunderbolt goal from debutant Christian Pander secured a 2-1 win for the Germans in the friendly match. Pundit Chris Waddle said afterwards: 'Overall, Germany gave us a football lesson. It just seems to be getting worse.' Just how much worse would become apparent when Croatia came to town later that year.

AUGUST 23

Two England full-backs were born on this day, exactly 101 years apart. The first was Jesse Pennington, born today in 1883 and nicknamed 'Peerless Pennington'. He was a left-back and one of West Bromwich Albion's greatest ever players, and a one-club man. He played 25 times for England, captaining the side on one occasion, but he achieved notoriety in 1913 when he was offered £5 to throw a West Brom game. Instead of taking the money Pennington called in the police and had the would-be briber Pascoe Bioletti arrested.

Glen Johnson would have no need to take a £5 bribe, even inflation corrected. The England right-back who shares his birthday with Pennington is now the most expensive England full-back in history having been bought by Liverpool for a sum reported to be around £18m, of which he would have been due a cut. Perhaps he will be able to afford to buy his own toilet seat.

AUGUST 24

William Slaney Kenyon-Slaney was an Eton and Oxford graduate, a decorated soldier and veteran of the Battle of Tel el-Kebir, the Member of Parliament for Newport in Shropshire, and a competent cricketer. He also liked his football and was the player who scored the first ever goal in international football. Kenyon-Slaney, who was born on this day in 1847 and played his club football for Wanderers, played in only the second ever international match between England and Scotland. The first fixture in 1872 had been a 0-0 draw so when Kenyon-Slaney scored in the 4-2 win at the Oval it was not only England's first ever goal, but also the first ever in an international fixture.

Michael Thomas also knows something about scoring crucial goals, for it was his last minute goal that clinched the most dramatic title win in English football history for Arsenal against Liverpool in 1989. Thomas was born today in 1967 and represented England twice in the late eighties.

AUGUST 25

Stuart Pearce was the 999th player to be capped by England when he was first called up in 1987 and went on to become one of the national side's most important players throughout the nineties, despite his penalty miss in the semi-final in the 1990 World Cup. Now forging a career as manager of the England under-21 team, Pearce took his first steps into coaching on this day in 1999 when he was brought in by FA technical director Howard Wilkinson to help train the England under-18 side. He was due to be involved with the team for a friendly against Switzerland in September 1999 but his good form for West Ham meant he earned a surprise recall to the England senior team by Kevin Keegan. He did take to the bench with the under-18s in October.

Bruce Russell, born today way back in 1859, was, like Pearce, also an England left-back, although his international career lasted for just one match: a 5-0 win over Wales in 1883.

AUGUST 26

Today in 1994 the Football Association began the search for the first ever technical director for the senior England set-up. 'We want players to have a higher technical ability and our coaches to reach improved standards,' FA chief executive Graham Kelly said. 'The new man would sit at the top of the pyramid and ensure all the England teams played the same way so players would be comfortable when they made the step up. (This) is something that every other country has had for some time,' he said. 'If, say, Terry Venables wanted to do particular things with defensive players, or wanted to introduce a certain type of player at international level, the co-ordinator would ensure the ideas were brought in and worked on lower down.' Former Leeds boss Howard Wilkinson eventually got the job.

Glenn Hoddle was preparing for his first match as England boss against Moldova today in 1996. Amid a raft of injury problems, Hoddle called up Everton player Andy Hinchcliffe for the first time. He played seven times for England, all under Hoddle.

AUGUST 27

Nat Lofthouse was one of the greatest players of his day and has the stats to back it up. In just 33 England appearances Lofthouse scored 30 goals, an incredible return and one of the best goals per game ratios of any post-war England international. The Bolton player, who never played for another club and was born on this day in 1925 was famous for his FA Cup exploits as well. He played in two finals, and both times the weight of public support was behind his rivals. In the first, in 1953, he scored but still lost as Stanley Matthews won a hugely popular first medal with Blackpool. In the second, in 1958, his Bolton team faced Manchester United, just months after the Munich air crash. The public was desperate for a fairytale story for United but Lofthouse spoiled the script by scoring twice to win it for Bolton.

The first Englishman to score at the new Wembley Stadium was David Bentley. The former Arsenal youngster, born today in 1984, netted for the England under-21s against Italy in a 3-3 draw.

AUGUST 28

When Bill Shankly paid out the enormous sum of £65,000 for Blackpool 19-year-old Emlyn Hughes in 1967, the great Liverpool boss justified the expense by claiming his latest signing was 'a future England captain'. As usual, Shanks was proved right. After being called up to the England squad by Sir Alf Ramsey in 1969, the Crazy Horse established himself in the Liverpool team and was used more and more by Ramsey. He was a member of the squad at the 1970 World Cup, but never made it on to the pitch. With England having a lean spell in the seventies, Hughes, born on this day in 1947, never played a World Cup match. In all he played 62 times for England, scoring once, and wearing the captain's armband 23 times.

AUGUST 29

After being sent off in England's second round defeat to Argentina in the 1998 World Cup, David Beckham was vilified in the press for his part in England's downfall with the *Daily Mirror* even printing a dartboard with Beckham's face in the middle. Today in 1998 the young winger played his first game after seeing red in France – away to West Ham with Manchester United. Hammers fans burned an effigy of Beckham outside an East End pub before pelting the United coach with missiles. During the game his every touch was booed as the home supporters made it abundantly clear who they blamed for England's latest World Cup failure. The match ended 0-0 but Becks went on to have one of his best ever seasons as United wrapped up a historic treble. Two years later, he was England captain and all was forgiven.

James Milner holds the record for the most appearances for the England under-21 side and would go on to win 61 senior caps on his way to winning almost every domestic honour on offer.. Today in 2008 Milner was snapped up from Newcastle by Aston Villa for £12m.

AUGUST 30

After he conceded a goal to Macedonia's Artim Šakiri direct from a corner in a Euro 2004 qualifier at Southampton's St Mary's Stadium, David Seaman was not picked again for the England team by Sven-Göran Eriksson. Today in 2003, after being ignored by Sven for a number of England games, Seaman admitted his international career was over after 75 caps.

Former England manager Sir Bobby Robson was collecting his P45 today in 2004 when Newcastle chairman Freddy Shepherd sacked him as manager after a dodgy start to the new season. Shepherd said he 'didn't want to be known as the man who shot Bambi', but he didn't hesitate in pulling the trigger on poor old Bobby. Newcastle have been on a downward spiral ever since.

AUGUST 31

'Once a blue, always a blue' – the words written on a t-shirt worn by England striker Wayne Rooney after scoring for his boyhood club Everton. Today in 2004 he became a hate figure among the Everton fans who had once idolised him when he signed for Manchester United. It was in an England shirt that Rooney had really shot to prominence, especially with his eye-catching performances at Euro 2004 which he took by storm until he was injured in the quarter-finals, with England's chances of success limping off with him. The £30m deal made him the most expensive England player after his United teammate Rio Ferdinand.

Another England regular who became hated by his own former fans is Ashley Cole. The left-back, a product of Arsenal's academy, left today in 2006 to sign for London rivals Chelsea, after throwing his toys out of the pram when the Gunners offered him 'only' £65,000 per week. Arsenal got £5m plus sulky French defender William Gallas in return for Cole.

ENGLAND
ON THIS DAY

SEPTEMBER

SEPTEMBER 1

After England came so agonisingly close to success in Euro 96 it was left to new England boss Glenn Hoddle to pick up the pieces and try to take the team forward to the World Cup in 1998. Today in 1996 Hoddle took charge of England for the first time, in a World Cup qualification match against Moldova. Nick Barmby, Paul Gascoigne and Alan Shearer got all the in the 3-0 win which also saw David Beckham make his England debut.

Five years later to the day and Beckham was the England captain wearing the armband when England enjoyed one of their best ever results – the 5-1 thrashing of Germany in Munich. Sven-Göran Eriksson's team needed something from the match to keep their World Cup 2002 qualification hopes alive but Carsten Jancker scored after just six minutes. Thereafter England went goal-crazy as a hat-trick from Michael Owen and goals from Steven Gerrard and even Emile Heskey wrapped up an amazing night for England fans.

SEPTEMBER 2

Before injuries began to take their toll on Michael Owen he regularly used to pop up and save England's blushes by scoring crucial goals. He did just that today in 2000 when Kevin Keegan's England took on World and European Champions France in Paris. Keegan had left Owen on the bench but the striker came on and reminded his manager what he had been missing by scoring with just five minutes left to secure a creditable 1-1 draw.

Steven Gerrard and Peter Crouch both scored their tenth England goals today in 2006 when England played minnows Andorra in a Euro 2008 qualification match at Old Trafford. Making a mockery of the 'there are no easy international games' cliché, England netted five without reply against the part-timers, with a brace each from Jermain Defoe and Crouch and one for Gerrard.

SEPTEMBER 3

Gerry Francis only ever won 12 England caps, but for eight of those matches he captained the side. He was first handed the armband for a friendly against Switzerland in Basle on this day in 1975. It was only his fifth appearance for England but he didn't disappoint and helped England to a 2-1 win thanks to goals from Kevin Keegan and Mick Channon.

Wolves legend Billy Wright captained England a record 90 times and was the first ever player to represent his country 100 times. Billy died on this day in 1994 aged 70.

SEPTEMBER 4

England hit Luxembourg for six today in 1999 at Wembley in a Euro 2000 qualifier. Newcastle midfielder Kieron Dyer made his international debut in the match but it was the more established players who stole the limelight. Skipper Alan Shearer had a field day against the bricklayers and bakers of the Luxembourg defence and scored the only hat-trick of his international career. Steve McManaman scored his first goals for England on his 25th appearance, bagging a brace, while Michael Owen chipped in with the final strike in injury time. It was the ninth time England had faced Luxembourg and the stats back up the argument that these tiny nations bring little to the international football scene. The record over the nine games reads, England won nine, scored 47 goals and conceded just three.

Only one England manager can point to a 100 per cent winning record in his time in charge of the Three Lions. Of course, it helps (statistically at least) that Sam Allardyce only took charge of one game: a 1-0 win over Slovakia on this day in 2016. The ex-Bolton boss would be forced to leave the job just weeks later after *The Telegraph*'s undercover sting.

SEPTEMBER 5

Despite being labeled 'as daft as a brush' by England manager Bobby Robson, Paul Gascoigne was called up to Robson's England squad for the first time on this day in 1988 for a friendly against Denmark.

Three months after being knocked out of the World Cup by Argentina, England were looking for a positive result today in 1998 in their first Euro 2000 qualification match, away to Sweden. Things started well as Alan Shearer scored after just two minutes from a free kick but from there on it was downhill as Andreas Andersson and Johan Mjällby each scored to give the hosts a 2-1 win. Even worse for England was that Paul Ince was sent off after 65 minutes for two bookable offences.

SEPTEMBER 6

Terry Butcher provided England fans with one of their most iconic images today in 1989 in a World Cup qualifier against Sweden. After a clash of heads with a Swedish player Butcher had to have makeshift stitches on the wound on his head. As the match went on and Butcher continued to head the ball his shirt and bandages became covered with blood but he helped England hold on to a draw. At half-time manager Bobby Robson told his players: 'Have a look at your skipper. Let none of you let him down.' Singapore-born Butcher told the *Guardian* afterwards: 'I was never going to quit. No Englishman would do that.' He even still has the shirt: 'My wife washed it,' he said. 'It actually washed up quite well.'

Colombian goalkeeper René Higuita stunned England fans on this day in 1995 in a friendly at Wembley. Jamie Redknapp hoisted an aimless cross-shot in to the Colombian goalmouth and instead of catching the ball Higuita cleared the ball by jumping on his hands and acrobatically clearing the ball with his feet – his famous 'scorpion kick'. Terry Venables said: 'I have only one word to describe it: extraordinary.'

SEPTEMBER 7

The England team engendered perhaps the best piece of commentary ever broadcast. No, not Kenneth Wolstenholme's 'They think it's all over', but Norwegian radio commentator Bjørge Lillelien's impassioned outburst after Norway defeated England for the first time on this day in 1981. After the 2-1 victory Lillelien cried: 'Lord Nelson! Lord Beaverbrook! Sir Winston Churchill! Sir Anthony Eden! Clement Attlee! Henry Cooper! Lady Diana! Maggie Thatcher – can you hear me, Maggie Thatcher! Your boys took one hell of a beating! Your boys took one hell of a beating!'

Another England defeat was also being celebrated by their unfancied opponents today in 2005 when Northern Ireland pulled off a 1-0 win over England in a World Cup qualifier at Windsor Park in Belfast. David Healy's goal inflicted the only defeat England suffered under Sven-Göran Eriksson in any qualification match. It was the first time Northern Ireland had beaten England since 1972.

SEPTEMBER 8

From the moment he burst onto the scene at Everton as a 16-year-old, Wayne Rooney looked like the best natural talent England had produced since Paul Gascoigne. And on this day in 2015 Rooney scored his 50th goal for England – a penalty against Switzerland – to become his country's all-time leading scorer, breaking Sir Bobby Charlton's record.

After the euphoria of England's World Cup campaign in Russia, the Three Lions were brought back down to earth on this day in 2018 by a defeat to Spain at Wembley in their first match in the new Nations League tournament. Marcus Rashford had given England an early lead, but Spain hit back with goals from Saul Niguez and Rodrigo Moreno to win 2-1. England eventually made it to the semi-finals, where they lost to Holland.

SEPTEMBER 9

England lost 3-1 to West Germany in a friendly on this day in 1987, with Gary Lineker netting for the Three Lions. Substitute Neil Webb became the 1,000th player to be capped by England when he came on. After Webb retired the former Nottingham Forest and Manchester United midfielder got a job as a postman until he began working as a football pundit.

As a young player coming through the ranks at Liverpool, Michael Owen seemed to be the perfect package: a pacey striker with an insatiable appetite for goals and a level-headed character. Today in 1997 he proved he wasn't a complete goodie-two-shoes when he was sent off while captaining the England under-18 side against Yugoslavia.

SEPTEMBER 10

Despite being a talented footballer, Stan Collymore's inner demons robbed him of many of his peak years and probably stunted his England career. He won just three caps, the last was today in 1997 against Moldova.

The first real signs that Fabio Capello was making a big difference to the England team came today in 2008 when he masterminded a fantastic 4-1 win over Croatia in a World Cup qualifying match in Zagreb – the scene of England's miserable 2-0 defeat under Steve McClaren two years before. The Italian coach sprang a surprise by starting with young Arsenal winger Theo Walcott wide on the right. It proved to be an inspired choice as the speedy youngster scored a hat-trick (becoming the youngest player ever to do so in an England shirt) while the other boy wonder Wayne Rooney grabbed the other goal. The result put England in pole position in their qualifying group. Capello said: 'The players played like they do in training – technically well and with courage. This is the start. But let's not get carried away. We have just started. It is the second game of the qualifying round. It is a good performance, a good result, but it is nothing.'

SEPTEMBER 11

The debacle that was the construction of the new Wembley Stadium began on this day in 2000 when Australian firm Multiplex signed the deal to build the new stadium for a maximum cost of £326.5m, with the, in hindsight, laughably ambitious target of the 2003 FA Cup final as the opening match. That target was soon dropped as financial delays, disputes with contractors and even blackmail and death threats dogged the project from start to finish. The stadium was eventually opened four years late and £450m over budget.

Arsenal, Middlesbrough and Aston Villa player Paul Merson made his England debut on this day in 1991 in a friendly against Germany at Wembley. Paul 'the Person' Merson started the match among the substitutes but with England 1-0 down and chasing the game, manager Graham Taylor threw him on. Paul was unable to affect the result and England lost yet another match to the Germans. Merson went on to win a further 21 caps, scoring three goals.

SEPTEMBER 12

Until Steve McClaren took the crown, Graham Taylor was the most mocked and derided England manager in history. His disastrous reign began today in 1990 when his team took on Hungary in a friendly match at Wembley. Taylor handed the England captaincy to Gary Lineker and his new skipper led by example and scored the only goal of the game as England won 1-0.

The FA were displaying a bit of cross-sport support today in 2005 when England cricketers became heroes by winning the Ashes. To celebrate the achievement, Test sponsors and Wembley energy suppliers Npower arranged for the Wembley arch to be lit up through the night. 'We felt lighting the Wembley arch was a fitting tribute to the outstanding cricket that we have seen from both teams this summer and an excellent way to celebrate an England win,' said Kevin Peake of Npower.

SEPTEMBER 13

Lancashire lad Sam Wadsworth had a promising career on the horizon with Blackburn Rovers until the First World War intervened and young Sam volunteered for military service aged just 17. After four years watching the horrors of war close up in the trenches with only the knowledge that he would one day return and play for Rovers to keep him going, he came home and Blackburn dumped him. 'My heart was broken. My life's dream had gone with the wind. I was very bitter after nearly five years' service. It was not very nice treatment,' he said much later. But he fought back and eventually earned a contract with Huddersfield, winning the FA Cup and three league titles with the club. In 1922 he went from being Blackburn Rovers reject to England international when he was picked to play against Scotland, even captaining the side in a later match. Wadsworth was born on this day in 1896 and passed away in September 1961 aged 64.

SEPTEMBER 14

The humble penalty kick: scourge of England, masterminded by Germany, invented by an Irishman and first seen today in 1891. In order to stop the excessive hacking that was spoiling many-a-game, a goalkeeper from Northern Ireland called William McCrum came up with the penalty kick as a way to stop cheating. The first ever player to step up to the 12-yard spot was John Heath of Wolverhampton Wanderers who slotted it home en route to his side's 5-0 thrashing of Accrington Stanley at Molineux on this day in 1981. England fans have been suffering ever since.

One of England's brightest talents of the modern age made his international debut on this day in 1988. Bobby Robson selected the young Paul Gascoigne for his England squad to face Denmark in a friendly at Wembley. Neil Webb scored the only goal of the game in which Gazza first pulled on an England jersey in anger after coming off the bench.

Deutschland
England
1 : 5
Olympiastadion
München
01.SEP.
2001
DIE BUNDESLIGA
S.A.F.C.
ROVERS FC

SEPTEMBER 15

Today in 1998 it looked like England had its next bright young thing, when 18-year-old Darius Vassell came off the bench to score two injury-time goals to give Aston Villa a last-gasp 3-2 win over Stromsgodset in the Uefa Cup. Vassell was a regular in the England under-18 team and would go on to make 22 appearances for the Three Lions. He would hang up his boots in 2012 after a stint at Leicester City.

Danny Mills joined Vassell in the 2002 World Cup squad, ably filling in for the injured Gary Neville at right-back and went on to make 19 appearances for England, all of which were away from Wembley, a modern-day record. On this day in 2004 the Manchester City defender was reportedly squaring up to manager Kevin Keegan after he took offence to the former England boss's assertion that the City defenders – and not Keegan's gung-ho tactics – were responsible for the club's poor performances that season.

SEPTEMBER 16

Although undoubtedly a supreme talent, Wayne Rooney often struggled with his temperament on the pitch in his early days, with a habit of falling foul of refereeing decisions after letting his frustration boil over into bad tackles and mouthing off to officials. It emerged today in 2005 that Rooney was seeing an anger-management expert to try to calm him down. His England and Manchester United teammate Rio Ferdinand told *The Guardian*: 'His temperament is always there to be questioned because he plays on the edge. He wouldn't be the same player if you took it away. I know that's a cliché, but it's true.'

Rooney's one-time England strike partner Michael Owen has always been more level headed. Today he was drawing more plaudits when he scored on his European debut for Liverpool in a Uefa Cup tie against Celtic in Glasgow on this day in 1997. The young striker got Liverpool's first and England teammate Steve McManaman grabbed a spectacular second as the reds drew 2-2.

SEPTEMBER 17

After being forced out of the England job by his barmy comments about disabled people, Glenn Hoddle went from being the coming man of football management to a man who needed to rebuild his career and reputation from scratch. Today in 1999 he was linked with the first job since his sacking with rumours he was to take over at Reading, where he lived. In the end he didn't take the job and pitched up at then-Premiership Southampton soon afterwards.

One of Hoddle's former charges in the England team, David Beckham, spoke out about his omission from the England squad by Steve McClaren for the first time today in 2006. 'I would be lying if I said I wasn't disappointed. It's a terrible feeling not playing for England after ten years of being involved. I still believe I have got two or three more good years in me. I have got a burning desire to prove him wrong,' he said. And prove him wrong he did, earning a recall soon afterwards.

SEPTEMBER 18

Peter Shilton, England's most capped player, was born on this day in 1949. The goalkeeper who played for Leicester, Stoke, Nottingham Forest and Southampton won 125 caps for England, and would have won a lot more had he not shared the goalkeeping jersey with Ray Clemence. He was between the sticks for three World Cup tournaments but will forever be remembered as the man who 5ft 5in Maradona managed to out-jump to score the Hand of God goal.

Sol Campbell is another England player born on this day who knows a thing or two about heartbreaking defeats to Argentina. Sol thought he had scored a last-minute winner in the World Cup 98 clash only for the referee to rule it out for pushing in the box. Six years later against Portugal at Euro 2004 exactly the same thing happened again. He came so close to being the hero twice, yet in 73 games for England, he scored only one goal that wasn't disallowed, against Sweden at the 2002 World Cup.

SEPTEMBER 19

The last time England enjoyed stability in the goalkeeping position was when David 'Able' Seaman held the jersey. Despite being caught off his line by Ronaldinho in 2002, Dave, who was born today in 1963, was a generally solid performer for England, notching up 75 caps in a 14-year international career.

While West Germany and the unified Germany have inflicted many a painful defeat on England, the Three Lions never lost to East Germany in four meetings. The last was a friendly today in 1984 at Wembley. Captain Marvel Bryan Robson scored the only goal of the game after 82 minutes on his tenth appearance for the national side.

SEPTEMBER 20

He was the best manager England never had. Brian Clough as boss of the national side would have been either a runaway success, or a complete disaster, and you couldn't rule out the fact that he might actually start a war – this was after all the man who labelled the Juventus team 'cheating bastards' after they knocked his Derby County side out of the European Cup. He was interviewed for the top job in 1977 after Don Revie's defection but the interview was merely to assuage public opinion and he was never seriously in the running for the post which went to Ron Greenwood. Clough died on this day in 2004, aged 69.

After England failed to qualify for the 1978 World Cup it was up to Greenwood to get the England set-up back on track. Today in 1978 the Three Lions took on Denmark in the first qualification match for the European Championships. A high-scoring game, skipper Kevin Keegan gave England a two-goal lead within 23 minutes. The Danes hit back and levelled the score with two goals in three minutes. Bob Latchford and Phil Neal added two more for England while a late strike from Per Røntved ensured a nervy finish for England who held on to win 4-3.

SEPTEMBER 21

In a match against Portugal in May 1947 Tommy Lawton scored after just 17 seconds, beginning a thrashing that would end 10-0. In his next match for the national side, a friendly against Belgium in the Heysel Stadium in Brussels, Lawton was at it again, and scored just 34 seconds after kick-off as England won 5-2.

England's humiliating 6-3 defeat at Wembley by Hungary in 1953 was hailed as a watershed moment in football: England had finally been beaten on home soil by a foreign team. But in actual fact, that had already happened four years earlier, on this day in 1949 when Ireland beat the Three Lions 2-0 in a friendly at Goodison Park thanks to goals from Con Martin and Peter Farrell. In a bid to play down the result, some of the papers held on to the notion that England were still unbeaten by any team outside of the British Isles.

SEPTEMBER 22

Bobby Robson took charge of the England team for the very first time today in 1982 when the national side took on Denmark in a qualifier for the 1984 European Championships. Robson immediately changed things around and dropped former captain Kevin Keegan. Newcastle fans were incensed and even spat on the man who would one day manage their team. In the match Trevor Francis scored twice in a 2-2 draw.

When Robson became Newcastle manager in 1999 one of his priorities was to plug the famously leaky Magpies defence but it wasn't until 2003 that he signed former Leeds defender Jonathan Woodgate. Woody was then sold on to Real Madrid in 2004 in what looked like a dream move. As usual though, Woody was injured when he signed and had to wait until today in 2005, more than a year after the transfer to make his debut. It was a complete disaster as he first scored an own goal and was then sent off. 'F**k me, what a debut!' was his response.

SEPTEMBER 23

England failed to win the race to host the 2006 World Cup and today in 2000 the cost of the failed bid was revealed to be almost £11m, nearly a third of which came from lottery funds. Nearly £500,000 of the money was used to pay 1966 heroes Sir Bobby Charlton and Sir Geoff Hurst to front the doomed bid. The bid document itself came in at £880,000.

'In any other team in the world if a striker had scored 30 goals in their domestic league, he would be a certainty for his national side...' The words of former Sunderland striker Kevin Phillips who was an unused substitute at Euro 2000. Today in 2000 he lined up against his rival for an England berth Michael Owen when Sunderland took on Liverpool at Anfield. Both players scored one each in the match which was a 1-1 draw.

SEPTEMBER 24

Eddie Hapgood, a pre-war Arsenal player with more than 400 appearances for the Gunners as a full-back, also played for England 30 times. The one-time milkman who was born on this day in 1908, made his international debut in a match against Italy in Rome, but it would be a subsequent clash with the Italians that made Hapgood more famous. He was captain for the infamous 'Battle of Highbury' match when World Champions Italy arrived to take on England at Arsenal's ground in the so-called real World Cup final. Hapgood himself suffered a broken nose as England overcame a barrage of fouls from the Azzurri to win 3-2.

Much later Steve Foster, also born today in 1957, would also find fame thanks to Arsenal. The central defender who won three England caps in 1982 under Bobby Robson, was the Luton Town captain when the Hatters pulled off a 3-2 win over the Gunners in the League Cup Final at Wembley in 1988.

SEPTEMBER 25

Stan Mortensen is famous for the hat-trick he scored in the 'Stanley Matthews' FA Cup Final in 1953 but the Blackpool legend also made a rather strange entrance in international football. He was named as England's reserve for a wartime fixture against Wales at Wembley on this day in 1943. During the match Wales defender Ivor Powell had to go off injured, but Wales had no reserve to replace him. With England 4-1 up and cruising, both captains agreed Mortensen could come on in Powell's place. England won 8-3. So the man who went on to score 23 goals for England actually made his international debut for Wales.

After violent clashes between rival fans at the Euro 2004 qualifier between England and Turkey at the Stadium of Light, the respective FAs decided to work together to try to avoid trouble at the return fixture in Istanbul. Today in 2003 officials from the FA travelled to Turkey to discuss the game. Eventually it was decided that no England fans would be allowed to attend the match.

SEPTEMBER 26

England played Denmark for the first time ever today in 1948 in a friendly match in Copenhagen. The uninspiring 0-0 draw saw Sunderland forward Len Shackleton make his international debut, the first of just five caps for the charismatic striker. It was also the last time Tommy Lawton ever played for England. The striker had an incredible record for his country, in 23 official matches he scored 22 goals. He also won 23 unofficial caps during the Second World War, netting 24 times in those games.

With 86 caps under his belt, former Crystal Palace and Arsenal defender Kenny Sansom holds the record for the most England games for a full-back. Kenny was born on this day in 1958.

SEPTEMBER 27

After England limped out of Euro 2016 with that humiliating loss to Iceland, boss Roy Hodgson resigned and the nation turned to Sam Allardyce as the new manager. It was the culmination of a long managerial career for the former Notts County, Bolton, West Ham and Sunderland boss who said when he was appointed: 'It is no secret that this is the role I have always wanted.' But sadly for 'Big Sam' the dream was over after just 67 days when he was forced to stand down on this day in 2016. He had been caught up in a sting operation by *The Daily Telegraph* who filmed him explaining to undercover reporters posing as businessmen how to 'get around' rules on player transfers involving third party ownership – as well as mocking his predecessor Hodgson. He apologised immediately, but the FA said his conduct was 'inappropriate' with chairman Greg Clarke saying his position had become 'untenable'. And so he was out, with a single match under his belt as England boss – a 1-0 away win in Slovakia.

SEPTEMBER 28

Walter Winterbottom was the first ever England team manager. His first match in charge of the team was on this day in 1946 when England took on Ireland in a Home Championship match at Windsor Park in Belfast. He had a start most bosses can only dream of as his side destroyed the Irish 7-2, with a hat-trick from Middlesbrough forward Wilf Mannion.

Horatio 'Raich' Carter scored the first goal of the match – it was the first to be scored by any England player since the end of World War Two. The match was also the international debut of Billy Wright. George Hardwick skippered the side that day – it was the last time any player has worn the armband on his debut.

SEPTEMBER 29

Not only was Sir Stanley Matthews the best player of his day and a hero to thousands of Blackpool and Stoke City fans, he was also a key figure for England, and had a top-level playing career that lasted for more than 30 years. He made his England debut on this day in 1934 aged 19. Typically he scored as England beat Wales 4-0 at Ninian Park in Cardiff. Incredibly, he was still playing for his country more than two decades later – his last cap came against Denmark in Copenhagen in May 1957, 22 years after his first.

Matthews was only one of a number of players making their international debuts in the match. Cliff Britton, John Barker, John Bray, Ray Bowden and Raymond Westwood all wore the Three Lions shirt for the first time.

SEPTEMBER 30

Bill Perry was made famous in the Stanley Matthews FA Cup Final of 1953 when he scored the last-minute winner for Blackpool from a cross from Matthews to give the Seasiders a 4-3 win after a thrilling match. Although Perry was born in South Africa, his father was a Londoner and in 1955 he was handed the first of three caps he won for England. In his second appearance he scored twice in a 4-1 win over Spain at Wembley. Perry passed away on this day in 2007 aged 77.

In 2000 Peter Taylor was the coming man on the English managerial scene. After success as the England under-21 boss and manager of Gillingham, Taylor was handed the job of taking over from Martin O'Neill at then-Premiership club Leicester City. He was being talked up as a future England boss and did take charge of the side once in 2000, famously handing David Beckham the England captaincy for the first time. Today in 2001 any talk of him landing the top job with England was swatted away when he was sacked as Leicester boss with the club rooted to the foot of the table.

ENGLAND
ON THIS DAY

OCTOBER

OCTOBER 1

An FA Services XI took on Belgium in a wartime tour match today in 1944, winning 3-0. Walley Barnes and Ted Drake scored either side of a Philibert Smellinckk own goal in another unofficial match. Turning out for England was Frank Soo of Stoke City, the first ever mixed-race player to play for England at any level. Born of Chinese and English parentage, free kick specialist Soo never received an official England cap, but did play in nine wartime games.

Wayne Rooney scored the first goals of his professional career today in 2002, bagging two in Everton's 3-0 Carling Cup win over Wrexham. Rooney's emergence that year terrified the late journalist Steven Wells in the *Guardian*, who compared the 16-year-old to an Amazonian crocodile: 'Look at his eyes! Have you ever seen deader eyes? Even on a dead person? Even on, like, a dead person with no eyes? They say that the eyes are the windows of the soul – but looking into Wayne Rooney's reptilian pits is like staring into Nietzsche's abyss. There is no humanity there, or compassion. There's only the message, beamed loud and clear: "I outlived the dinosaurs and I will outlive your kind too, human. And my offspring will lay their eggs in your children's flesh-stripped bones. Now come a bit nearer the water's edge so I can bite yer frickin' legs off."'

OCTOBER 2

Future England boss Don Revie made his debut for the Three Lions on the pitch today in 1954, scoring England's second goal in a 2-0 win over Northern Ireland. Revie went on to make six appearances for England, scoring four goals. England's other goalscorer that day was another debutant, Johnny Haynes, who scored the first of his 18 goals for England.

Revie was in the goals again exactly a year later, as he starred in England's 5-1 win over Denmark in Copenhagen, scoring twice. Bolton legend Nat Lofthouse also bagged a brace with Bristol Rovers centre forward Geoff Bradford adding the fifth on his only ever England appearance.

OCTOBER 3

Billy Wright kitted up for the Three Lions today in 1951 for the first of a record 70 consecutive appearances. The Wolves legend would not miss another national team game until he hung up his boots in 1959 against the USA, but today suffered a disappointing 2-2 draw with France at Highbury. Tottenham's outside-left Leslie Medley was on song for England, scoring the equaliser after Walter Winterbottom's men found themselves 2-1 down after 20 minutes.

In 1962 England today first dipped their toe into the European Championships, playing France in a qualifier for the 1964 tournament at Hillsborough. England had given the initial 1960 competition a miss and were held to a 1-1 first-leg draw, with Ron Flowers scoring a second-half equaliser from the penalty spot. The return leg the following February saw England crash out of the competition, losing 5-2 in Paris.

OCTOBER 4

The outbreak of World War II in 1939 initially put the brakes on both international and domestic football in England, but soon enough the nation was back watching and playing its favourite sport. Although not officially recognised as full internationals England and Scotland kept up their rivalry, meeting several times during the conflict, including a match at Wembley today in 1941 where Winston Churchill made an appearance to boost morale. A report at the time said: 'A terrific welcome was roared as he shook hands with the players,' as England would win 2-0.

Today in 1952 saw England take on Northern Ireland in a Home Championship clash in Belfast. Nat Lofthouse scored his tenth England goal in the first minute, but a Charles Tully brace put the Irish ahead. Burnley outside-left Billy Elliott was on hand to save the day however, dancing his way to a 90th minute equaliser.

OCTOBER 5

Today in 1997 as England were preparing for their crucial World Cup 98 qualifier against Italy in Rome, Glenn Hoddle invited a 17-year-old Michael Owen to train with his squad. Owen had just broken into the Liverpool first team and starred in that summer's Fifa World Youth Championship in Malaysia, scoring three goals for the England under-20 side. He had long been talked about as the next big thing in English football and by the end of the season he had firmly established himself in the England set-up.

Sven-Göran Eriksson had to delay naming his England squad today in 2003 as the Rio Ferdinand drug test saga rolled on. With the FA yet to announce whether the Manchester United centre-back would be available for selection, Gary 'Red Nev' Neville took it upon himself to act as an Arthur Scargill-type figure and called for the players to boycott their next match, the crucial Euro 2004 qualifying game against Turkey.

OCTOBER 6

David Beckham finally achieved redemption today in 2001 for his red card against Argentina in 1998. After three years of being subject to boos across the country, the midfielder turned in his best performance in an England shirt, covering ever blade of grass against Greece during England's final World Cup 2002 qualifier. England had been making extremely hard work of the Greeks, trailing 2-1 in injury time when Beckham stepped up to fire a trademark free kick home and send the Three Lions to Japan and South Korea.

One of Beckham's predecessors on England's right flank was also making history today, as Stanley Matthews bagged a second-minute goal against Northern Ireland in 1956 to become England's oldest-ever scorer at the grand old age of 41 years and 248 days. Clean-living Stan attributed his longevity to being a vegetarian teetotaller, finally quitting top flight football as a 50-year-old in 1965 and afterwards claiming he had retired 'too early'.

OCTOBER 7

Where to start with England's clash against bitter rivals Germany today in 2000? Captain Tony Adams' 60th Wembley appearance which is more than any other player? Another disappointing England loss? Nope, the game is probably most famous for being England's swansong at the original Wembley Stadium. On a wet, grey day in London, the twin towers didn't get the send off they deserved: Dietmar Hamann's speculative free kick somehow found it's way through David Seaman's grasp. The Arsenal stopper blaming David Beckham for handing the ball to the German before he was ready was one of his poorer excuses.

Minutes after the final whistle England manager Kevin Keegan was on the Wembley toilet, reflecting on his tactical choices that afternoon, such as placing Gareth Southgate in central midfield. As honest as he was emotional, KK decided there and then that enough was enough and quit on the spot. 'I have just not been good enough,' he admitted as he washed his hands and walked away.

OCTOBER 8

England's under-21 team were delayed by two hours today in 1996 when their European Championship qualifier was held up by a bomb scare. An over-eager steward at Molineux saw a foil-wrapped package and feared the worst. Following a controlled explosion it emerged that the parcel was no more than a sandwich. England's performance was somewhat less than explosive, as they drew 0-0 with Poland. Apart from keeping an eye on your lunch, the other lesson of the day was never let Aston Villa defenders take penalties whilst in England colours: Riccardo Scimeca missed from the spot, three months after his club teammate Gareth Southgate's poor effort against Germany in Euro 96.

David Beckham was an angry man after becoming the first England player to be sent off twice for his country, following two quick yellow cards in England's 1-0 win over Austria today in 2005. 'The first one was harsh, but the second one was even harsher,' he fumed. 'I couldn't understand it. I don't think it was a sending off at all.'

OCTOBER 9

Perhaps the only man more popular than Alan Shearer in Newcastle, Wor Jackie Milburn, died today in 1988. After being plucked from a life down t'pit, Milburn went on to score 238 goals for Newcastle and also bagged a very respectable ten goals in 13 games for England. He also never got Newcastle relegated, so scores another win over his successor in the Newcastle and England number nine shirt there. His death also fell on the anniversary of his England debut, as Milburn scored for England today in 1948 in a 6-2 win over Northern Ireland.

Today in 2004 David Beckham was on the receiving end of another controversial carding when he received a yellow after a foul on Wales defender Ben Thatcher. With England coasting to a win, Azerbaijan next up in the World Cup 2006 qualifying campaign and Beckham carrying an injury, the England skipper claimed that his card was deliberate, as it earned him a suspension for a game he knew he would miss anyway. 'It was deliberate,' boasted Mr Posh Spice. 'I am sure some people think that I have not got the brains to be clever, but I do have the brains.'

OCTOBER 10

Today in 1999 England's famous 'left-sided problem' was no nearer a solution after Kevin Keegan gave Steve Guppy a run-out in a friendly with Belgium at the Stadium of Light in Sunderland. To the surprise of very few people, the 30-year-old Leicester City winger was not the answer and he never featured for the national team again. Another debutant that day who has gone on to make more of an impact was Frank Lampard, as England won 2-1 with Alan Shearer and Jamie Redknapp providing the goals.

There was another lacklustre display from England at Wembley today in 1999, as they drew 0-0 with Bulgaria. Manager Glenn Hoddle's typically nonsensical judgement of the game was that 'A 0-0 draw is sometimes worse than a 1-1 draw.'

OCTOBER 11

Is there anything that encapsulates the grit of English football more than a bandaged England captain, blood pouring out of his head as he stoically leads his charges to victory? Today in 1997 Paul Ince was the man in the role that Terry Butcher had made famous eight years earlier, as he led a disciplined, heroic England performance in Rome to pick up the point that Glenn Hoddle's men needed for qualification to the 1998 World Cup. Ian Wright came oh-so close to scoring at the death, striking the post, but in the end a draw was enough to condemn Italy to the play-offs. Brian Glanville saluted Ince's restraining job on Gianfranco Zola, saying, 'Zola a ghost, Ince heroic.'

An inspirational skipper was just one of the things that Steve McClaren needed today in 2006 as England travelled to Croatia. Add to that list a right-back without designs on his own goal and a 'keeper that can cope with backpasses. A 2-0 European Championships qualifying loss today offered the first signs that Steve McClaren was hopelessly out of his depth, experimenting with a 3-5-2 formation and seeing Gary Neville's weak backpass bobble over Paul Robinson's foot to provide the Christmas bloopers DVD market with another England highlight.

OCTOBER 12

The man who possibly did more than anyone to ensure England won the World Cup died today in 1993. Not Bobby Moore, Geoff Hurst or even Sir Alf, but Tofik Bakhramov, or 'the Russian linesman' as he will forever be known. That tag is actually misleading, as he hails from Azerbaijan, where they even named the national stadium after him. Described by Brian Glanville as 'a man with the flowing grey hair of a concert violinist,' Bakhramov was reportedly asked on his deathbed how he knew the ball was over the line in 1966. He uttered one word: 'Stalingrad.'

England's under-21 team were also up against West Germany today and didn't need the help of a linesman with a grudge, as they squeezed past their rivals 5-4 on aggregate to win the 1982 European Championships, with Gary Owen and Justin Fashanu among the goalscorers.

175

OCTOBER 13

Did he not like that. Graham Taylor took his England team to Rotterdam today in 1993 for a do-or-die World Cup qualifier against the Dutch, complete with a documentary film crew in tow. The Channel 4 crew were on hand to get Taylor's every reaction to a series of controversial refereeing decisions, as England went down 2-0 and saw their hopes of reaching the 1994 World Cup virtually disappear. 'Will you say to the fella, the referee has got me the sack,' Taylor said to the linesman at the final whistle. 'Thank him ever so much for that, won't you?'

In 2004 England visited the Tofik Bakhramov Stadium in Azerbaijan, a day after the anniversary of this country's favourite official's death. Ranked at 116th in the world, Azerbaijan shouldn't have given England too many problems, but they toiled to a 1-0 win thanks to a first-half Michael Owen strike.

OCTOBER 14

England faced Norway in a World Cup qualifier today in 1992 and it was left to Paul Gascoigne to provide the pre-match international diplomacy. When he was asked by a Norwegian camera crew if he had a message for England's upcoming opponents Gazza responded with 'Yes. F**k off Norway,' before turning around and running away laughing. The game finished 1-1, with David Platt scoring for England and Gazza picking up a yellow card.

England were again flattering to deceive against lowly opposition today in 1998 as they travelled to Luxembourg. After five minutes of this European Championship qualifier Luxembourg won a penalty, but Dany Theis shot wide. England bucked their ideas up, winning 3-0 after goals from Michael Owen, Alan Shearer and Gareth Southgate in another unconvincing performance.

THE WALLY WITH THE BROLLY: STEVE McCLAREN CHECKS OUT AS ENGLAND MANAGER

OCTOBER 15

The Fabio Capello revolution really began to gather pace today in 2008 when England's 3-1 win in Belarus marked the first time that they had won their first four matches in a World Cup qualifying campaign. As Emile Heskey won his 50th cap, Scousers Steven Gerrard and Wayne Rooney provided the goals, with the Manchester United man scoring twice.

England played their 250th match today in 1949, downing the Welsh 4-1 at Ninian Park. Stan Mortensen scored the opener, which was England's 750th goal and Jackie Milburn took care of the rest, netting a hat-trick.

OCTOBER 16

It was one gaffe too many for David Seaman on his 75th and final appearance today in 2002. England were playing Macedonia at St Mary's in Southampton and after only ten minutes the Arsenal 'keeper let Artim Šakiri score direct from a corner. David Beckham soon equalised, but England were again behind as the Macedonians, buoyed by their positive start, tested a shaken Seaman at every opportunity. Steven Gerrard made it 2-2 but England couldn't find a winner. Leeds striker Alan Smith's last minute red card compounded England's woes that night. Seaman finished his career with 75 caps, having played in the 1998 and 2002 World Cups and the European Championships in 1996 and 2000.

England and Scotland met today in 1945 in a wartime international. These games were not recognised as full international matches and Scotland would be thankful for this, as they were tonked 8-0 with Tommy Lawton bagging four, including a ten-minute first half hat-trick at Maine Road.

OCTOBER 17

England's dreams of qualification for the 1974 World Cup were ended today in 1973, thanks to a 'clown'. Alf Ramsey's men had backed themselves into a corner where only a win at Wembley would do against Poland and found themselves a goal down with 30 minutes left. Allan Clarke soon equalised, but the second goal would come thanks to the heroics of Jan Tomaszewski in the Polish goal. In the television studio Brian Clough labelled the Pole as a clown due to his unorthodox technique, but we all know who was laughing last that night. England's failure meant the beginning of the end for Sir Alf, who never got England through a World Cup qualifying campaign, with England hosting the competition in 1966 and going through as holders four years later.

The sun began to set on another England manager's regime today in 2007, when Steve McClaren took his team to Moscow to face Guus Hiddink's Russia. To compensate for the plummeting temperatures the game was played on a plastic pitch; England prepared by training on a similar surface at Blessed Thomas Holford Catholic College in Altrincham. With 20 minutes to go it looked as though this move was paying off, as England led thanks to a Wayne Rooney goal, but a late Roman Pavlyuchenko brace was another nail in McClaren's coffin.

OCTOBER 18

Legendary Fulham and England forward Johnny Haynes died in a road accident today in 2005. Haynes was the first footballer to be paid £100 a week and scored 18 goals in his 56 caps for his country, 22 of which he skippered the Three Lions in. Domestically, he was a one-club man, turning out for Fulham 658 times.

England got their 1947/48 Home Championship campaign off to a winning start as they beat Wales 3-0 at Ninian Park today in 1947. First-half goals from Tom Finney, Stan Mortensen and Tommy Lawton were enough to give England the win as they began a successful defence of their title.

OCTOBER 19

Bobby Charlton and Jimmy Greaves had to tussle over the match ball tonight in 1960, after they both scored hat-tricks in England's 9-0 demolition of Luxembourg. Bobby Smith added two more and captain Johnny Haynes also netted during one of England's easier 1962 World Cup qualifying matches.

Legendary England skipper Billy Wright set a new world record for the most number of caps today in 1957, when he pulled on the England colours for the 86th time. Wright led his men to a 4-0 win over Wales at Ninian Park, with his successor as England captain Johnny Haynes scoring twice. Don Howe, who later returned to the England fold as Terry Venables' assistant manager in the mid-90s won the first of his 23 caps that day, sharing his debut with Eddie Hopkinson and Bryan Douglas.

OCTOBER 20

Word Champions England swept aside Northern Ireland today in 1966 with a 2-0 win at Windsor Park in their match that acted as both a Home Championship and Euro 68 qualifier. The same XI that took care of West Germany earlier that year were too strong for the Irish, with goals coming from Roger Hunt and Martin Peters as Bobby Charlton made his 75th appearance.

Northern Ireland put up a better fight today in 1926, as they held the Three Lions to a 3-3 draw at Anfield. England were on the ropes at half-time, trailing 3-1, but second-half strikes from Joe Spence and Norman Bullock rescued the Home Championship tie for England, as they would go on to secure a share of that season's title with Scotland.

OCTOBER 21

Today in 2000 England were in a right mess. Still reeling from Kevin Keegan's resignation in the Wembley toilets two weeks earlier, the FA were struggling to find a quality replacement for him. FA chief exec Adam Crozier attempted to buy some time by installing a temp in the form of a 67-year-old that could never remember his player's names. Crozier's hopes were dashed though, when Newcastle chairman fat Freddy Shepherd refused to play ball and let the FA approach Bobby Robson over a sensational return to the national team.

Back to 1953 now, as England clung on to their belief that they were still the greatest side in the world. A month later any delusions of grandeur would be firmly laid to waste by the Mighty Magyars of Hungary, but today they faced a Fifa all-star XI at Wembley to celebrate the FA's 90th anniversary and the warning signs were there. It took a last minute Alf Ramsey penalty to salvage a 4-4 draw as Laszlo Kubala stole the show, with one somewhat patronising report at the time exclaiming, 'Who said the Europeans can't shoot!'

OCTOBER 22

England's greatest ever goalkeeper Gordon Banks' career was prematurely ended today when the Stoke stopper crashed his car on the way home from a physiotherapy session. After losing control and ending up in a ditch, Banks lost the sight in his right eye and the loss of binocular vision meant that he had no hope of pulling off saves such as the legendary stop from Pele in the 1970 World Cup.

Bolton stalwart Nat Lofthouse scored his 30th and final England goal today in 1958 when the Three Lions romped to a 5-0 win over the USSR. Johnny Haynes also added a hat-trick to give England their first win over the Soviets in the fourth clash between the two nations.

OCTOBER 23

The stars were out at Wembley today in 1963, when England took on a Rest of the World XI in celebration of the 100th anniversary of the FA. Facing Alf Ramsey's men were the likes of Alfredo di Stéfano, Eusébio, Ferenc Puskás and Denis Law, but it was Lev Yashin in goal that took the plaudits that night, as the Soviet 'keeper had one of the games of his life, but was unable to prevent Terry Paine and Jimmy Greaves scoring as England sent the 100,000-strong crowd home happy, winning 2-1.

Chelsea forward George Mills made an instant impact on the international scene today in 1937, scoring a hat-trick on his debut, as Northern Ireland were put to the sword 5-1 in Belfast. Wolves legend Stan Cullis also made his first appearance in this Home Championship clash.

OCTOBER 24

England could legitimately call themselves world champions today in 1908, as Great Britain picked up the Olympic gold medal at the White City stadium in London. In what could be a good omen for 2012, the British side was exclusively made of Englishmen and faced a rampant Denmark side that had clocked up 26 goals in their last two matches, with Sophus Nielsen scoring ten in their 17-1 win over France in the semi-final. In front of 8,000 fans Frederick Chapman and Vivian Woodward scored in a 2-0 win for the Brits, but the *Official Olympic Report* believed that the score-line 'rather flattered the winners who did not show real international form. Denmark, on the other hand, displayed the greatest vigour and determination with far more pace and dash than against France.'

England's selectors can't have been too impressed with the 0-0 draw against Northern Ireland today in 1925, as four of the five England debutants never again turned out for their country. Claude Ashton, Sam Austin, George Armitage and Francis Hudspeth are all members of the one-cap club.

OCTOBER 25

International football was back today in 1919 after a five-year hiatus while war raged on the continent. England looked as though they hadn't missed a beat, as Huddersfield centre forward Jack Cock scored after only 30 seconds against Ireland at Windsor Park in Belfast. James Ferris equalised for the Irish who had only just got the hang of playing England before the war, having won their last two meetings at the 31st time of asking.

England booked their place in the 1962 World Cup today in 1961 when they downed Portugal 2-0 at Wembley. Goals in the first ten minutes from John Connelly and Ray Pointer were enough to see off Eusébio and company, and England would not then have to play another qualifier for 11 years, as they would automatically enter the next two tournaments as hosts and then winners.

OCTOBER 26

The seeds for the England team and international football as we know it were laid today in 1863 when the FA was founded in the Freemason's Tavern in Great Queen Street in London. Ebenezer Cobb Morley may sound like a cruel workhouse boss from a Dickens novel, but he convinced 11 clubs to create a standardised set of rules for clubs across the country to follow. The rest, as they say, is history.

By today in 1938 the FA was going strong and celebrated their 75th anniversary with a match against a Fifa European Select XI at Highbury. Freshly crowned World Cup winners Italy provided four players, wisely none of the XI that were present at the infamous 'Battle of Highbury' four years earlier. Goals from Willie Hall, Tommy Lawton and Len Goulden gave the birthday boys a 3-0 win and further strengthened the English belief that they were untouchable at the top of the international game.

OCTOBER 27

The England women's team were celebrating their biggest-ever win today in 2005 when they romped to a 13-0 win over Hungary in Tapolca. Former Arsenal striker Kelly Smith led the way, scoring a hat-trick, with seven of her teammates also getting on the scoresheet in front of only a smattering of supporters in the ancient spa town.

Paul Gascoigne made an ill-advised venture into management today in 2005 when he became boss of Kettering Town. Although he would claim at the time 'I won't be making this club look like a circus,' when he was appointed, he might as well have been dressed in a top hat and tails, as he did his best ringmaster impression, with rumours over his alcohol addiction resurfacing as he refused to accept the fact he had been sacked a month later.

OCTOBER 28

England's under-17s fought back from 2-0 down to beat Spain 5-2 and win the FIFA U17 World Cup in India today in 2017. Golden Boot winner Rhian Brewster and Phil Foden were among the scorers as Steve Cooper's side were crowned world champions, raising hopes of a new 'golden generation'. Their success came after England's under-20s also celebrated a World Cup win of their own earlier that year, with their 1-0 win over Venezuela coming in the first global final appearance by any England side since 1966.

England went down 3-2 to Sweden under the twin towers at Wembley today in 1959. This was the fourth loss in six games for Walter Winterbottom's team as they struggled to keep up with the changing pace of international football. Sweden meanwhile, were beginning to carve out a niche as one of England's bogey teams, recording their second win over England and having only lost to the Three Lions twice since.

OCTOBER 29

England's Aston Villa legend Billy Walker was born today in 1897. Walker found the net nine times in 18 games for England in the 1920s and was the first Englishman to score at Wembley Stadium, when he fired home against Scotland in 1924. Domestically he finished his career in 1934 as Villa's all-time top goalscorer, a record he holds to this day with 244 goals and would later move into management, winning the FA Cup with Sheffield Wednesday in 1935 and Nottingham Forest, where he spent 21 years as boss, in 1959.

The BBC were muckraking today in 2007 when *Panorama* investigated several senior Fifa figures whilst 'examining whether England can expect 'fair play' from Fifa" in bidding for the 2018 finals. As in the case of the infamous bung investigation from the same programme in 2006, very little came of it.

OCTOBER 30

The Don Revie era kicked off today when the former Leeds manager took charge of the Three Lions for the first time. Handing debuts to Gerry Francis and David Thomas, Revie's England beat Czechoslovakia 3-0 at Wembley in this Euro 76 qualifier, with Micky Channon opening the scoring before Colin Bell added a late brace. England would go on to record six consecutive clean sheets in Revie's first half-dozen games. Revie took in 29 matches as England manager, starting brightly, but ending in failure to qualify for the 1978 World Cup and the controversy of him ditching England for a highly paid job in the Middle East.

A year later England were again facing the Czechs; the tables were turned in Bratislava, as Zdeněk Nehoda and Peter Gallis gave them a 2-1 win over England. The game had originally kicked off the night before, but heavy fog forced the players off after only 17 minutes.

OCTOBER 31

The job of being England's second choice goalkeeper is often a thankless task. Just ask Peter Bonetti who was Gordon Banks' ill-fated understudy in the 1970 World Cup or the likes of the talented Nigel Martyn who never got a chance to strut his stuff on the world stage. Ian Walker, who was born today in 1971, is most famous for letting Gianfranco Zola beat him at the near post in England's 1-0 World Cup 98 qualifying match in 1997.

Adam Crozier left his position of chief executive of the FA today in 2002 to join the Royal Mail. The former Saatchi and Saatchi man was appointed by the FA to provide some modern-day business nous to the often arcane corridors of power in English football and was the man responsible for bringing in England's first foreign manager when he gave Sven-Göran Eriksson the nod in 2001.

ENGLAND
ON THIS DAY

NOVEMBER

NOVEMBER 1

Steve McClaren's 18-match tenure in the England hot-seat had more than its fair share of embarrassing moments, but his ultimate humiliation surely came today in 2006 when he was sacked by his spin-doctor Max Clifford. 'It's proving to be a waste of my time and his money,' said the self-anointed PR guru, proving he knew a sinking ship when he saw one. 'I can't operate properly for Steve if I don't know what he's doing all the time.' Don't worry Max, none of us knew what he was doing either.

How McClaren would have enjoyed being England manager in the 1920s. With 50 years of international experience behind them, England were ahead of the rest of the world, as proved when they dispatched Belgium 6-1 at Highbury today in 1923. Kenneth Hegan of Corinthians netted twice on his debut in the second contest between the two nations.

NOVEMBER 2

The freshly crowned world champions were held for the first time today in 1966 as Czechoslovakia came to Wembley and drew 0-0 with the same XI that had lifted the Jules Rimet trophy three months earlier.

England played their 300th match on this day in 1955, coasting to a 3-0 win over Northern Ireland. Wolves forward Dennis Wilshaw bagged a brace in this Home Championship clash. This would be England's only win in the competition that year, as all four home nations finished with identical records, winning, losing and drawing once. Goal difference was yet to factored in so the title was shared between England, Scotland, Wales and Northern Ireland.

NOVEMBER 3

The English tabloid press enjoy a 'special' relationship with the England team. One day they'll be waxing lyrical about how England will win the World Cup, and the next they're photoshopping the manager's face onto a root vegetable. Jeff Powell of the *Daily Mail* is more vocal than most and today in 2000 gave his damning verdict on the FA's appointment of a foreign coach: 'So, the mother country of football, birthplace of the greatest game, has finally gone from the cradle to the shame. We've sold our birthright down the fjord to a nation of seven million skiers and hammer throwers who spend half their lives in darkness.' Needless to say, Sven would have the last laugh, as Powell made a spectacular u-turn following the 5-1 win over Germany less than a year later: 'England are back,' he joyfully proclaimed. 'Back with such a vengeance that our bright young men and their courteous Swedish manager may indeed have changed the face of the game.'

These days Ian Wright, who was born today in 1963, is more familiar to fans for his passionate musings as a pundit, but in his pomp he was one of English football's most feared strikers, emerging from non-league football to win 33 England caps and score nine goals for his country, while going down as an Arsenal legend.

NOVEMBER 4

Michael Owen was doing the two things that he does best today in 2001: scoring goals and getting injured. Owen was on the scoresheet twice for Liverpool as they beat their bitter rivals, and his future employers, Manchester United 3-1 at Anfield, but later twanged his hamstring for the umpteenth time and was forced to miss England's friendly with Sweden later that month.

Despite his history of injury woes, Owen has still managed to rack up over 85 caps for England, but his Liverpool teammate Rob Jones wasn't so fortunate. Right-back Jones, who was born today in 1971, looked set to become an England regular, but injuries limited him to only eight England appearances.

NOVEMBER 5

Emlyn 'Crazy Horse' Hughes made his England debut today in 1969 when he turned out in a friendly against Holland in Amsterdam. A late Colin Bell goal gave England the spoils and Hughes would later go on to be the only player capped in the 1960s, 70s and 80s as the Liverpool man when on to win 62 caps, skippering the side 23 times and scoring a single goal. After hanging up his boots Hughes became a captain on the BBC's *A Question of Sport* and he also named his daughter Emma Lynn, but don't hold that against him.

England played Northern Ireland at Goodison Park today in 1947, with a blockbuster finish resulting in a 2-2 draw. Trailing 1-0 with six minutes remaining Wilf Mannion and Tommy Lawton both struck quick-fire goals before Peter Doherty, proving he didn't get caught in possession nearly as much as his musical namesake, equalised in injury time. This left England to rue Mannion's 70th minute penalty miss.

NOVEMBER 6

Liverpool left-winger Alan A'Court's joy at a debut goal was short lived today in 1957 when England went down 3-2 to Northern Ireland at Wembley. Duncan Edwards was also on the scoresheet, netting his final goal for England before being tragically killed in the Munich air crash, but the Irish, led by the Blanchflower brothers, were too strong in this Home Championship contest.

A friendly in Budapest today in 1968 provided less excitement as England played out a 0-0 draw with Romania. Bob McNab of Arsenal made his debut, coming on after ten minutes when Tommy Wright went down injured.

NOVEMBER 7

As well as being the best rapper that the beautiful game has produced – yes, that includes you Andy 'Andrew' Cole – John Barnes, who was born in Kingston, Jamaica today in 1963, was one of the finest players ever to represent the Three Lions. Barnes won 79 caps and scored 11 goals for England, the best being his superlative effort against Brazil in the Maracanã in 1984 when he slalomed past the Seleção defence before rounding the 'keeper and slotting home.

The Liverpool left-winger shares a birthday with his former England teammate Mark Hateley who was born in 1961. Hateley blazed his way onto the international scene when he starred in the England under-21 team's winning European Championship campaign, scoring six goals in the knockout stages. This earned him a high-profile move to AC Milan, but with a return of eight goals in 32 England games, Hateley never quite lived up to his early promise in an England shirt.

NOVEMBER 8

Martin Peters, the other goalscorer on England's finest day, was born today in 1943. Peters only made his England debut three months before the 1966 World Cup final, but impressed Alf Ramsey enough to secure his place in the squad, playing in all but the first game of the tournament. The versatile West Ham midfielder would later go on to captain his country and scored 20 goals in his 67 games in an England shirt.

Along with Geoff Hurst and Bobby Moore, Peters was a member of the famous West Ham 'Academy of Football' that played such a huge role in the 1966 win. Another Hammers graduate is Joe Cole who was born today in 1981 and became an England regular after leaving West Ham for Chelsea in a £7m move in 2003, providing the highlight of England's lacklustre 2006 World Cup campaign with his stunning volley against Sweden.

NOVEMBER 9

QPR's jinking genius Rodney Marsh made his international debut today in 1971 as England drew 1-1 with Switzerland in a Euro 72 qualifier. Mike Summerbee scored his first and only goal for England and Marsh would only make nine appearances for his country as Alf Ramsey failed to find a regular place in his side for the unorthodox forward.

England took on Norway at St James' Park today in 1938, easing to a 4-0 win. Ronnie Dix scored on his only ever England appearance, and Millwall outside-left Reg Smith was also in on the debut goal act, bagging England's opening and closing goals in front of 39,887 Geordies.

NOVEMBER 10

Sven-Göran Eriksson took on his countrymen as England boss for the first time today in 2001 in a friendly at Old Trafford. Handing debuts to Trevor Sinclair and Danny Murphy, England went ahead through a David Beckham penalty, but were pegged back when Håkan Mild equalised on the stroke of half-time to ensure that honours were even in what would be Darren Anderton's final game for England. Sven faced his compatriots four times as England manager, notching up a conspiracy theory-friendly record of three draws and one defeat.

Walter Winterbottom's charges took on Wales at Wembley today in 1954 and had Chelsea striker Roy Bentley to thank, as his late hat-trick gave the Three Lions a 3-2 win. The Welsh led 1-0 with 20 minutes remaining after John Charles' opener, but Bentley's 18-minute treble ensured that England stayed on track for the Home Championship title. Bentley only played 12 times for England but managed an impressive nine goals.

NOVEMBER 11

England romped to Euro 88 qualification today in 1987, as they confidently dispatched Yugoslavia 4-1 in Belgrade. A blitzkrieg opening 25 minutes saw England go 4-0 up, thanks to goals from Peter Beardsley, John Barnes, Bryan Robson and Tony Adams. This meant that England easily topped their qualifying group, and headed off to the finals in West Germany with the usual heightened level of expectation.

The 1953/54 Home Championship also doubled up as the qualification group for the 1954 World Cup and today in 1953 England put one foot in the finals when they recorded a 3-1 victory against Northern Ireland. The Bolton Wanderers duo of Harold Hassall and Nat Lofthouse were responsible for the England goals, with Hassall bagging a brace on his final international appearance as the win meant England needed only to avoid defeat to Scotland to qualify for the tournament in Switzerland next summer.

NOVEMBER 12

Strictly speaking, England's clash with Argentina in Geneva today in 2005 was a friendly, but ever since Sir Alf's 'animals' rant in 1966, the Falklands War and a certain handball in 1986, the term 'friendly' doesn't apply between these two old rivals. England found themselves 2-1 down with five minutes remaining, but cometh the hour, cometh the man. Michael Owen, a man who knows a thing or two about scoring against Argentina, nodded in an 87th minute equaliser and then scored a sensational winner in injury time.

England took on Yugoslavia today in 1986 in a Euro 88 qualifier, easing to a 2-0 win. Gary Mabbutt scored his first goal for his country as Terry Butcher captained the side for the first time. Viv Anderson scored the opener, in what still remains the last England goal ever scored by a player sporting a moustache.

NOVEMBER 13

England's laboured attempts to qualify for Euro 2000 came to the boil today in 1999 when they faced the auld enemy in a play-off first-leg at Hampden Park. Kevin Keegan's men took the initiative early, racing to a 2-0 half-time lead in Glasgow, with Paul Scholes scoring both goals. A typically feisty game saw ten yellow cards distributed as England held on to their lead and put themselves in the driving seat for the return match at Wembley four days later.

England secured Euro 92 qualification today in 1991, when a 1-1 draw in Poland was enough win their group, ahead of Jack Charlton's Republic of Ireland team. England left it late though, needing a Gary Lineker leveller 13 minutes from time after Roman Szewczyk put the Poles ahead after half an hour, as Graham Taylor gave debuts to Andy Gray, Andy Sinton and Tony Daley.

NOVEMBER 14

Italy came to Highbury today in 1934 intent on adding the scalp of England to the World Cup crown they had won five months earlier. What ensured was one of the grittiest and bad-tempered matches international football has ever seen. In the first minute debutant Ted Drake broke Luisito Monti's leg and seconds later Carlo Ceresoli got his revenge by scything Drake down in the area, handing England a penalty which Eric Brook missed. The goals soon came though, as Brook scored two and Drake another, all in the first incident-packed 12 minutes. Both sides kept knocking several lumps out of each other, as ten-man Italy brought the score back to 3-2 with a brace from Giuseppe Meazza. England held on to win, leaving the *Times* to confidently assert that: 'The true verdict of the match, in appearances, is that England is still supreme in a game essentially her own.'

A 7-0 Wembley thrashing of Montenegro was a fitting way to celebrate England's 1,000th match today in 2019. Harry Kane's first-half hat-trick put them on their way, with the win booking the Three Lions' place at Euro 2020.

GEOFF HURST CLINCHES THE 1966 WORLD CUP WITH HIS THIRD GOAL OF THE GAME IN THE FINAL MINUTE OF EXTRA TIME

NOVEMBER 15

Under-21 boss Peter Taylor was installed as caretaker manager for England's clash with Italy in Turin today in 2000 and one of his first moves was to install David Beckham as skipper. One of his next, and far less successful, was to hand Seth Johnson his one and only England cap. A solitary goal from Gennaro Gattuso was enough to give the Italians a 1-0 win.

Also making their debuts were Liverpool duo Ray Clemence and Kevin Keegan, when England took on Wales in a World Cup 74 qualifier today in 1972. This was England's first World Cup qualifying game for 11 years, due to them hosting the event in 1966 and qualifying as winners four years later, but any cobwebs were soon swept away when Colin Bell struck in the first half to give the Three Lions a 1-0 win in Cardiff.

NOVEMBER 16

England's Home Championship match against Northern Ireland today in 1938 was the Willie Hall show. The Spurs inside-forward scored a first-half four-minute hat-trick, which still remains the quickest treble that international football has ever seen. He wasn't done there though, adding another two goals after the break, with his five-goal haul equalling the single game record, as England romped to a 7-0 thrashing.

The Steve McClaren era was inching closer to its inevitable conclusion today in 2007 when England took on Austria in Vienna. The Euro 2008 co-hosts were not supposed to provide too many problems for McClaren's men, but a lone goal from Peter Crouch was all they could conjure up in a 1-0 win. Making his debut was Scott Carson and his clean sheet was enough for Steve McClaren to start the young Liverpool stopper in their next game, the crucial Euro 2008 qualifier against Croatia five days later. We all know what happened next...

NOVEMBER 17

Having played themselves into a corner during the 1994 World Cup qualifying campaign England took on San Marino, needing a seven-goal win and a slip-up from Holland to make it to the USA. Facing a country with a population that wouldn't fill Stoke's Britannia Stadium, it took only eight seconds for England to fall behind after Davide Gualtieri latched onto a misplaced Stuart Pearce back pass. A 7-1 win couldn't hide England's embarrassment and meant Graham Taylor's men could worry about where to go on holiday the following summer. The game, played in Bologna, also attracted the lowest ever attendance for an England game since the 19th century, with only 2,378 witnessing San Marino's finest moment in international football. Brian Glanville later recalled that 'The press box, largely occupied by English journalists, erupted in incredulous laughter.'

In 1999 England met the auld enemy for the last-ever time at the original Wembley Stadium, as the Scots sought to overturn their two-goal deficit from the Euro 2000 play-off. Despite a first-half goal from Don Hutchison, Keegan's men held on for a narrow 2-1 aggregate win, meaning that the Scots would be staying at home that summer, but they at least had the satisfaction of victory in their final game at the twin towers.

NOVEMBER 18

It was the end of several eras today in 1998 when England beat the Czech Republic 2-0 at Wembley. Little did he know at time, but Glenn Hoddle was taking charge of his last England game before he decided to air his views on reincarnation. Also turning out for the last time were Ian Wright, Dion Dublin and Paul Merson. Merse marked his final cap with England's second goal after Darren Anderton's opener, before making way for debutant Lee Hendrie.

Tommy Lawton was one of England's greatest ever goalscorers, notching up 22 goals in 23 games in a war-interrupted international career, but today in 1947 the 28-year-old striker made a shock move from Chelsea to Third Division Notts County for a record fee of £20,000.

November 19

Stan Mortensen knew a thing or two about hat-tricks. He had the misfortune to see his 1953 FA Cup Final treble overshadowed by Stan Matthews' performance in what has gone down as 'The Matthews Final', but today in 1947 no-one was stealing his limelight, as he put three past Sweden in a 4-2 win in a friendly at Highbury. Tommy Lawton, fresh from his big-money transfer the day before scored the other in the days before Sweden established themselves as a bogey team for England, who have only beaten them twice since.

Today in 2008 England locked horns with Germany for the 27th time and recorded a 2-1 victory at the Olympiastadion in Berlin. Matthew Upson had given England a half-time lead with his first ever England goal, but a mix-up between John Terry and Scott Carson led to an equaliser from Patrick Helmes. The England captain made amends five minutes from the end though, as he headed home a winner to give England their first win over their greatest rivals since the famous 5-1 triumph in 2001.

November 20

Jimmy Greaves was in the goals today in 1963 as he led the line by scoring four in England's 8-3 rout of Northern Ireland at Wembley. Despite this drubbing the Irish would take a share of the title that season as the competition finished in a three-way tie between England, Scotland and Northern Ireland as goal difference was yet to be introduced as a tie-breaker.

England took on Wales at Stamford Bridge today in 1929 and again had their scoring boots on, winning 6-0. Middlesbrough striker George Camsell scored his second hat-trick of the calendar year, and would go on to score a ludicrously good 18 goals in nine England appearances.

NOVEMBER 21

It was another one of those days where every Englishman is put through the mixer on a rollercoaster ride of emotions that ends in crushing disappointment today in 2007. England took on Croatia at a soggy Wembley, knowing that a draw would be enough to see them through to Euro 2008. The Croats, meanwhile, had other ideas. Steve McClaren had inexplicably chosen the inexperienced Scott Carson in goal for England's most important match in years and the young 'keeper had an absolute horror show in the pouring rain, as England went 2-0 down in the first 15 minutes. A David Beckham inspired fightback in the second half saw England draw level and it looked as though everything was going to be alright, but Mladen Petrić scored a third for Croatia and England could not find another equaliser as McClaren looked on from under his umbrella, looking hopelessly out of his depth and waiting for that inevitable phone call from his bosses to call time on his tenure.

Another England manager was reaching the end of his regime today in 1962, but Walter Winterbottom's last match in charge was a far more enjoyable affair. Winterbottom left his job after England beat Wales 4-0 as he stood aside for Ipswich boss Alf Ramsey to take the reins.

NOVEMBER 22

It was the morning after the night before for Steve McClaren in 2007. In a rare instance of decisiveness and guts, the FA were quick to boot the man dubbed 'second choice Steve' from Soho Square. The day had already started badly for McClaren, as he awoke to find the press had given him a new nickname after he sheltered from the rain during the previous night's game: the wally with the brolly.

A future England boss would make his debut today in 1979, as Glenn Hoddle made his bow against Bulgaria, finding the net in a 2-0 win.

NOVEMBER 23

Another England manager bit the bullet today, as Graham Taylor quit in 1993. This came in the wake of England's failed 1994 World Cup qualification campaign that culminated in the humiliation of conceding a goal to San Marino after only eight seconds. With a smorgasbord of vegetable-related puns following after each disappointing result, Taylor was given a rougher ride by the tabloid press than most in the England job.

Jimmy Greaves notched up England's 1,000th goal today in 1960 when he netted in the second minute against Wales at Wembley. Greaves added another as England went on to a 5-1 win, with Bobby Charlton, Bobby Smith and Johnny Haynes joining him on the scoresheet.

NOVEMBER 24

Believe it or not, but when Terry Venables stepped down as England manager after Euro 96 one of the favourites to replace him was former Three Lions skipper and then-Middlesbrough boss Bryan Robson. As Captain Marvel's career in the dug-out progressed it became apparent that he shouldn't be let anywhere near the England team, with even Bradford City, who he took charge of today in 2003, proving to be too much of a challenge as he would only last one season at Valley Parade, in which he oversaw their relegation to the third tier of English football.

The fabled 'Academy of Football' at West Ham lost one of its young England starlets today in 2000, as Rio Ferdinand joined Leeds United for £18m, a world record fee for a defender at the time. At Elland Road Rio cemented his place in the England team and following his impressive performances in the 2002 World Cup was on the move again, joining Manchester United for £29m, regaining the title of the world's most expensive defender that he had lost to Juventus' Lilian Thuram in 2001.

NOVEMBER 25

English football was rocked to its foundations today in 1953 in what was probably the most significant match the Three Lions have ever played. The creators and self-anointed kings of the sport were handed a footballing lesson by Hungary in their own backyard, as the Mighty Magyars of Puskás, Hidegkuti and company demolished England 6-3. England were outplayed, outthought and outclassed by the Hungarians, with centre-half Syd Owen saying it was 'like playing people from outer space.' Billy Wright was tasked with handling Puskás, but got nowhere near him, causing journalist Geoffrey Green to say in the *Times*: 'Wright went past him like a fire engine going to the wrong fire.' For the first time, England needed to take a long, hard look at themselves in the mirror, as the times were-a-changing.

England's most capped player made his international bow today in 1970, as Leicester City goalkeeper Peter Shilton turned out against East Germany at Wembley. Goals from Franny Lee, Martin Peters and Allan Clarke ensured that Shilts was off to a winning start, as England triumphed 3-1.

NOVEMBER 26

England's 1950 World Cup loss to the USA was seen more as a one-off embarrassment that the 1953 Hungary reverse, so it didn't take long for the press and public alike to convince themselves England were still the best in the world. A 5-0 win over Belgium at Wembley today in 1952 was greeted with the assured newspaper headline: 'Recovery complete: England on top again.'

Bobby Charlton was handed the big red book today in 1969, as the Manchester United forward was featured on *This is Your Life*. That season was Charlton's last as an England player, as he would leave the pitch for the final time when he was substituted in the 70th minute of England's loss to West Germany in the 1970 World Cup quarter-final, with the Three Lions 2-1 up at the time.

NOVEMBER 27

Len Shackleton, one of English football's great characters, died aged 78, today in 2000. The showboating Newcastle and Sunderland forward was nicknamed 'the clown prince of football' but only turned out five times for the national side, as the selectors didn't dare take a risk on the man who later said in his autobiography that: 'There are so many things wrong with British football and so few things right that I can honestly state that I have no desire to be capped again.'

France were the visitors to Wembley today in 1957, as future England boss Bobby Robson made his first appearance on the pitch, scoring twice in a 4-0 win. Tommy Taylor of Manchester United provided the other two goals in what would his, Roger Byrne's and Duncan Edwards' final game for England before the trio would tragically lose their lives in the Munich air disaster five months later.

NOVEMBER 28

Alf Ramsey scored his first England goal today in 1951, as he struck from the penalty spot in England's 2-2 draw with Austria in a friendly at Wembley. Arsenal's cricket playing outside-right Arthur Milton made his one and only England appearance that day, becoming the last man to play cricket and football for his country. Ramsey scored three goals in his 32 England games, all from the penalty spot, with his coolness under pressure and ability to anticipate the goalkeeper earning him the nickname 'the General'.

Stanley Matthews brought up his half-century today in 1956 making his 50th England appearance in a friendly against Yugoslavia. Tommy Taylor came on as a substitute for the injured Johnny Haynes and scored twice to give his side a 3-0 win.

NOVEMBER 29

Viv Anderson became the first black player to be selected for England today in 1979 when Ron Greenwood played the Nottingham Forest right-back in a friendly against Czechoslovakia at Wembley. England won 1-0 thanks to a second-half Steve Coppell strike after a mistake by Czech 'keeper Pavol Michalik, as Anderson would go on to establish his place in Greenwood's side, winning 30 England caps.

Steven Gerrard will go down in history as one of England's greatest ever players, but today in 1998 not even those in the Kop at Anfield recognised the skinny 18-year-old as he prepared to make his Liverpool debut. He later recalled: 'All the subs were applauded when Gérard Houllier sent us to warm up. Well, nearly all. When I ran towards the Kop I could almost hear them saying: "Who's this skinny little twat?"'

NOVEMBER 30

It all started today. When FA secretary Charles Alcock arranged for the finest players from England and Scotland to have a kick-about today in 1872 he must have had no idea what he had created. The first official international football game took place in foggy conditions that caused a 20-minute delay at Hamilton Crescent in Scotland in front of 4,000 fans, each paying a shilling for the privilege of watching a game that changed the world. England's tactic was to dribble the ball until tackled, Scotland's was to pass the ball around. The two approaches cancelled each other out in a 0-0 draw – the only goalless stalemate between international football's two oldest rivals until 1970.

Gareth Southgate was appointed England manager today in 2016, after passing his four-match audition to succeed Sam Allardyce. A so-so spell in the Middlesbrough dugout was followed by an up-and-down stint as England U21s boss and meant his appointment was questioned in some quarters, but these critics were silenced during England's run to the World Cup semi-finals in 2018.

ENGLAND
ON THIS DAY

DECEMBER

DECEMBER 1

Sir Stanley Matthews played 54 times for England, but never in a more exciting match than on this day in 1937. England took on Czechoslovakia in a friendly match at White Hart Lane. Sir Stan netted three goals – his only international hat-trick – as England beat the Czechs 5-4.

Len Shackleton had the talent to play for England a lot more than the five caps he earned, but he was considered too much of a loose cannon to bring into the national team set up, with manager Walter Winterbottom complaining: 'If only Len would come half-way to meet the needs of the team there wouldn't be many to touch him.' Always a player who believed football should be about entertainment, one of the England selectors who refused to pick him said it was 'because we play at Wembley stadium, not the London Palladium.' Shack did finally score for his country on this day in 1954 when England beat West Germany 3-1 at Wembley. It was his first England goal on his last appearance.

DECEMBER 2

England hosted Switzerland for the first time ever in a football match today in 1948. The game had been due to be played the previous day but heavy fog in London meant the match was postponed. Although the match was played at Highbury, it was the first time in 16 years that no Arsenal players were in the starting line up. No less than five players made their international debut for England, one of them future World Cup winning manager Alf Ramsey who was then a right full-back playing for Southampton. England won the game 6-0.

Highbury was also the venue for a friendly against Hungary on this day in 1936. Arsenal striker Ted Drake scored a hat-trick on his penultimate England appearance as England won 6-2.

DECEMBER 3

After Steve McClaren's sacking as England boss the media began touting potential candidates for the job. Former Chelsea boss Jose Mourinho was soon in the frame and today in 2007 his advisor said he would be interested in the post. 'If he were approached he'd consider it, discuss it, negotiate, present his own ideas,' said Eladio Parames. 'It would be an honour. He likes English football, the people, the country and the players. It's something he'd consider but he's not trying to get the FA's attention.' He eventually took the manager's job at Internazionale while Fabio Capello took over as England boss.

One cap wonder watch! This time, it's Percy Humphreys. The former QPR, Notts County and Leicester player who was born today in 1880, played once for England against Scotland in 1903, in a team made up of players from 11 different clubs – the first time it had happened.

DECEMBER 4

England played their 200th official international match today in 1935, and what better way to celebrate the landmark game than by beating Germany? After the First World War, England had refused to play Germany for 12 years, but the two nations finally reconciled football-wise with a friendly in Berlin in 1930 (3-3). The return match finally took place on this day and two goals from George Camsell and one from Cliff Bastin gave England a 3-0 win over the Germans.

Another noteworthy aspect of the game was the amazing level of travelling support from Germany: an incredible 12,000 fans made their way across the English Channel and then on colour-coded trains up to London. With Hitler's Nazi regime already causing trouble with its anti-Semitic beliefs, staging the match at White Hart Lane with Tottenham's strong Jewish connections was perhaps an odd choice. Planned demonstrations never happened though and trouble was avoided, partly as the British government had banned Nazi symbols and swastikas from the game.

DECEMBER 5

A glimpse at what might have been today in 1956 for England fans. The national side took on Denmark in a World Cup qualifier at Wolves' Molineux ground, and the Danes were comfortably beaten 5-2. Manchester United youngsters Tommy Taylor, 24, and Duncan Edwards who was just 20 got all five goals: Taylor a hat-trick, Edwards a brace. Both players died in the Munich air crash two years later as both club and country were robbed of two fine young talents at a tragically early age.

Carlton Palmer has more England caps that Stan Bowles, Matt Le Tissier and Peter Osgood put together. Scarcely believable but true. The lanky midfielder from the Midlands was born today in 1965.

DECEMBER 6

England had no trouble dispatching France in a friendly match today in 1933 at White Hart Lane. George Camsell scored twice and Eric Brook and Thomas Grosvenor also netted in a 4-1 win over the visitors. Arthur Rowe, who would later lead Tottenham to their first ever First Division title as manager in 1951, made his one and only appearance for England in the game at his club stadium. Newcastle United's full-back David Fairhurst also made his one and only England appearance in this game, while for Willie Hall of Spurs, it was his first of ten caps.

Although England and the USSR were locked in the tense stand-off of the cold war during the sixties, the football show must go on and the Russians arrived in England on this day in 1967 to play a friendly at Wembley. Alan Ball opened the scoring after 23 minutes but the Russians hit back with two quickfire goals from Igor Chislenko just before half-time. Martin Peters preserved capitalist honour with 20 minutes left to play when he netted the equaliser.

DECEMBER 7

Two decades before Ferenc Puskás and the Mighty Magyars of Hungary humbled England at Wembley in 1953, the Austrian 'Wunderteam' arrived in England today in 1932, determined to be the first side from outside the UK to beat England on home soil, and they very nearly pulled it off. England went 2-0 up in the first half at Stamford Bridge through Jimmy Hampson while Eric Houghton and Sammy Crooks scored for the home side after the break. But the Austrians also netted through Zischek (twice) and Sindelar to make it 4-3 at the final whistle, and a nervy finish for England. They had come closer than most, but no cigar.

Father of the year 2009 John Terry was born today in 1980. The 'ard as nails Chelsea defender was made England captain by Steve McClaren and kept the armband following Fabio Capello's appointment as manager.

DECEMBER 8

England have only ever played at The Hawthorns twice, but West Bromwich Albion's home has been a happy hunting ground for the side on both occasions. On the first, England beat Ireland 2-0 in 1922, and in the second, on this day in 1924, they defeated Belgium 4-0 with two goals each from Joe Bradford and Billy Walker. Arsenal centre-half Jack Butler made his one and only appearance for England that day and in an odd quirk of fate later took charge of the Belgian side, overseeing their only ever win over England, in a friendly in 1936.

Real Madrid's Santiago Bernabéu hosted a friendly between Spain and England on this day in 1965 with a goal each from Roger Hunt and Joe Baker sealing a 2-0 win for Alf Ramsey's team. Leeds United's Norman Hunter came on for Baker and became the first player to make his England debut as a substitute.

DECEMBER 9

While the 6-3 tonking by Hungary at Wembley in 1953 is regarded as the first time England realised they had no divine right to win at football, a 4-3 defeat by Spain in Madrid in 1929 was the match that shook the unshakable belief for the first time. Today in 1931 England avenged the loss by thrashing Spain 7-1 at Highbury in a friendly with two goals each from Sammy Crooks, John Smith and Tosh Johnson, and another from Dixie Dean. It was all too much for Spanish goalkeeper Ricardo Zamora who was reportedly in tears at the end of the game having had to pick the ball out of his net seven times. 'What's Za-mora with you?' was the headline in the *Liverpool Echo* the next day.

England played Holland in a friendly today in 1964, Jimmy Greaves netting England's only goal in the 1-1 draw in Amsterdam. Alan Mullery made his debut for the national team in the match – the Tottenham midfielder would later become the first man to be sent off for England in a game against Yugoslavia.

DECEMBER 10

In 1921 25,000 paying spectators turned out to watch an unofficial match between Dick, Kerr's England and France. Concerned that the women's game might be getting more popular than the men's, the FA decided to ban women from using their pitches. Today in 1921 the women responded by meeting in Blackburn and forming the English Ladies FA.

Wembley was the venue for a friendly between England and Portugal on this day in 1969 which the World Champions won 1-0 thanks to a Jackie Charlton goal. It should have been 2-0 though as England were awarded a penalty. Manchester City's Francis Lee who holds the record for penalties scored in a single season (15) and was known as 'Lee One Pen', missed the spot kick, almost hitting the corner flag.

DECEMBER 11

Tottenham Hotspur centre forward Vivian Woodward had his shooting boots on today for an England amateur match against Holland. Woodward managed six goals in the game – the second time he had scored a double hat-trick for England after he managed eight against France in a 15-0 win in 1906.

A friendly against Bulgaria on this day in 1968 was a decidedly less goal-crazy affair with just one each scored in a 1-1 draw, Geoff Hurst netting for England. Manchester City midfielder Franny Lee, Everton goalkeeper Gordon West and Leeds United defender Paul Reaney all made their international debuts in this game.

DECEMBER 12

'Gareth Southgate, the whole of England is with you!' But it very nearly wasn't – the defender only made his England debut six months before Euro 96 kicked off. Terry Venables gave him his first cap in a friendly against Portugal at Wembley on this day in 1995. The match was a 1-1 draw; Steve Stone netted for England. Southgate had only four matches to get used to international football before Euro 96 in which he played every game, famously missing the penalty that put England out against Germany in the semi-final. He eventually won 57 caps.

The draw for the Euro 2000 tournament group stage was made today in 1999. England were drawn in group A against perennial rivals Germany, plus Portugal and Romania for the competition in Belgium and Holland. Asked if he was worried about Germany, Keegan said: 'Nein!' Adding: 'I'm really looking forward to it now. The players will look at that and say if we play to our potential we have got a good chance of going through. People at home will be rubbing their hands and saying "Let's get the show on the road"'.

DECEMBER 13

Perhaps in a bid to remind punters arriving late for football matches what they might miss, Bryan Robson wasted no time in getting the game going today in 1989. The England skipper scored the quickest ever goal in a professional match at Wembley Stadium when he netted with just 38 seconds on the clock as England took on Yugolsavia. Captain Marvel's goal helped England to a 2-1 win – their 100th victory under the twin towers of Wembley. The match was also a personal milestone for Tony Dorigo who was playing for his country for the very first time.

Nine years later and Bryan Robson was busy destroying the vast amount of credibility he built up as a player in his first managerial role at Middlesbrough. Meanwhile the nation had a new goal scoring hero: young Michael Owen picked up the BBC Sports Personality of the Year Award today in 1998, one day before his 19th birthday and almost entirely down to his wonder goal against Argentina at the World Cup.

DECEMBER 14

After the disastrous reign of Steve McClaren ended with England failing to qualify for Euro 2008, the FA decided to go all out in search of someone capable of getting the national side back on track. Today in 2007 Fabio Capello was appointed as the 12th manager of England. 'Fabio is a winner. His record over the last two decades speaks for itself,' said FA chief executive Brian Barwick. 'At every club he has managed, Fabio has won the league title and Sir Trevor Brooking and I were left in no doubt of his passion and commitment to bring that success to the England team.' Capello described the job as a 'beautiful challenge.'

Capello's homeland was the scene of probably the worst moment in Chris Waddle's career – apart from the 'Diamond Lights' single obviously. The England midfielder who missed a penalty in the semi-final against West Germany in Turin, was born on this day in 1960.

DAVID BECKHAM RECEIVES HIS 100th CAP FROM ENGLAND RECORD SCORER SIR BOBBY CHARLTON.

DECEMBER 15

The England under-21 team played their first ever fixture on this day in 1976 when they took on Wales at Wolverhampton Wanderers' ground, Molineux. Echoing the result of the first ever match the senior side played way back in 1872, the youngster could manage no better than an uninspiring 0-0 draw.

Things were far more entertaining today in 1982 when England hammered minnows Luxembourg at Wembley 9-0 in a Euro 84 qualifier. The result was a record win at Wembley for England and equalled Luxembourg's heaviest ever defeat, which was also inflicted by England in 1960. Former Watford and Milan striker Luther Blissett became the first black player ever to score for England in the game, netting a hat-trick. He never scored again for the national team.

DECEMBER 16

The England and Scotland rivalry is the oldest and one of the most fierce in football and things got a little tasty in the Euro 2000 play-off first leg match at Hampden Park in November 1999. England won 2-0 thanks to two goals from Paul Scholes but each side had five players booked during the game. While the fans might have enjoyed seeing their players get stuck into the opposition, Uefa took a rather different view and on this day in 1999 both England and Scotland were fined for 'improper conduct of the team'.

The words 'improper conduct' often go in the same sentence as the words 'Dennis Wise'. The snarly former Wimbledon and Chelsea midfielder played 21 times for England yet was surprisingly only ever booked once, in a friendly against Argentina in 2000. Wise, who was born today in 1966, scored on his England debut against Turkey in 1991 and nearly ten years later he played all three matches of England's disastrous Euro 2000 campaign under Kevin Keegan.

DECEMBER 17

Michael Owen was fast tracked into the senior England squad almost as soon as he broke into the first team at Liverpool. He only ever made one appearance for the England under-21 team, today in 1997 against Greece at Norwich's Carrow Road ground. Typically, he scored in the 2-2 draw.

Four years later to the day and Owen was celebrating again when he was awarded the prestigious Ballon d'Or award. He was the first English player to pick up the award since his Liverpool predecessor Kevin Keegan in 1979. The award capped a great year for Owen who won five trophies with Liverpool and scored a hat-trick in England's 5-1 win over Germany.

DECEMBER 18

Stanley Matthews was the first ever recipient of the European Footballer of the Year award, today in 1956. Incredibly, the Stoke, Blackpool and England legend was 41 when he picked up the first ever Ballon d'Or and still playing for club and country. He beat off the challenge of Real Madrid's Alfredo di Stéfano and Raymond Kopa of Stade Reims to win, but both went on the pick up the award in subsequent years. Since Matthews only three other English players have won the award, Bobby Charlton, Michael Owen and Kevin Keegan twice.

Sir Bert Millichip, the former West Bromwich Albion player and later chairman, who was chairman of the Football Association for 15 years, passed away on this day in 2002 aged 88. He presided over one of the most challenging periods in English football that encompassed the Heysel disaster and the rise of hooliganism, the breakaway of the Premier League and the bumbling reign of Graham Taylor. His lack of decisive action over Taylor's clearly failing regime and other issues earned him the sobriquet 'Bert the Inert'. Just ten weeks before Terry Venables was appointed England manager, Sir Bert said he would get the job 'over my dead body'.

DECEMBER 19

Former England captain Tony Adams fell foul of the law today in 1990 when he was sentenced to three months in prison for crashing his car while four times over the alcohol limit. The Arsenal centre-half publicly admitted he was an alcoholic in 1996 when he sought help. He went on to set up the Sporting Chance clinic to help other sportsmen with their addiction problems.

Rio Ferdinand later took Adams' place in the heart of the England defence, but he too was in trouble on this day in 2003. Following his missed drugs test, Ferdinand was today slapped with an eight-month ban and a £50,000 fine after his 'I forgot, honest guv', excuse didn't wash with the FA. PFA chief executive Gordon Taylor called the ban 'draconian' and Rio's club bosses at Manchester United reacted even worse: 'savage and unprecedented' said club director Maurice Watkins.

DECEMBER 20

These days it is rare enough for a Championship level player to be selected for the full England squad. Goalkeeper Reg Matthews, born today in 1933, was the first third division player ever to be capped by England when he made his debut against Scotland in April 1956. He was also the first Coventry-born footballer to play for the national side. He won five caps in total, all in 1956 but kept just one clean sheet, against Sweden in May of that year.

After four years with home-town club Coventry, Matthews signed for Chelsea in 1956, but probably not on the sort of wages that attracted fellow blues player Ashley Cole to the club. The two men share a birthday, but probably little else.

DECEMBER 21

John Frederick Peel Rawlinson, born today in 1860, had one of the most boring international careers of any England footballer. The goalkeeper who won the FA Cup in 1882 with Old Etonians and later became a barrister and a Member of Parliament, was called up just once for his country, for a friendly match against Ireland in Belfast in February 1882. It was Ireland's first ever international match and they were completely overwhelmed by England. The scoreline of 13-0 suggests Rawlinson had little to do between the sticks for England. He never played for his country again.

Horatio 'Raich' Carter had a much more eventful England career. The Sunderland inside-forward, also born on this day in 1913, was one of the biggest names in football in the pre-war period. Sadly his playing time was curtailed by the Second World War and he played just 13 times for England, scoring seven goals.

DECEMBER 22

Why is it, that in a country of 50 million people, England has consistently struggled to find one single player to play on the left of midfield? In 2004 in a friendly against his native Sweden, Sven-Göran Eriksson tried yet another option in the position that has become not so much a problem as a disability for England. Former Bolton and Celtic winger Alan Thompson, born today in 1973, was given 45 minutes to show what he could do. It obviously wasn't enough because he was never selected again.

Eddie Latheron, born today in 1887, only managed one more cap for England than Thompson but rather than not impressing enough to be recalled, Latheron's England career was halted by the First World War. After scoring on his debut against Wales in 1913 and then playing again in 1914, Latheron enlisted in the British Army. He was killed in the Battle of Passchendaele in October 1917, aged 29.

DECEMBER 23

Gareth Southgate, Chris Waddle, Stuart Pearce, David Beckham, Darius Vassell, Frank Lampard, Steven Gerrard and Jamie Carragher. Missing penalties for England is now a rich tradition all of its own and all these players are part of a club that isn't nearly as exclusive as England fans would like. The very first man to miss a spot-kick for England was Jimmy Crabtree. The former Aston Villa captain, who was born on this day in 1871, blazed over from 12 yards against Ireland in 1899, and so began the story of misery for England's penalty takers that continues to this day. Luckily for Jimmy, England still won 13-2 so it was not crucial in the outcome of the match.

DECEMBER 24

The Munich air crash was not just a tragedy for Manchester United, for one of Manchester City's most revered former players also perished in the disaster. Frank Swift, born today in 1913, was one of England's greatest ever goalkeepers and as well as keeping net for City for his entire professional club career, he was also capped 19 times. In 1948 he also became the first goalkeeper to captain England since Alexander Morten in 1873 when he took the armband for a famous 4-0 victory over Italy in Turin – the first time the Italians had been beaten at home for 14 years. In later life Swift became a journalist for the *News of the World* and was on duty covering Manchester United's European match when he was killed in Munich.

Crewe Alexandra manager Ernie Tagg once said of Stan Bowles: 'If Stan could pass a betting shop like he can pass a football, he would be all right.' Stan, born today in 1948, was one of the most talented players of the seventies, but he won just five England caps. 'I was happy playing for QPR,' he said in 2005. 'I played five times for England, for three different managers. Some say I got them all the sack.'

DECEMBER 25

It was the ultimate England versus Germany match-up, yet no one is exactly sure of the score, or even who was playing or how many joined in. Christmas Day 1914, and for one amazing day in the middle of the most horrific war the world had ever seen, the soldiers on both sides laid down their arms and emerged into no-man's-land, had a bit of a sing-song, exchanged some gifts, and then, like all groups of foreign people struggling to understand each other, resorted to having a bit of a kick-about.

It is extremely hard to pin down exactly what happened on that magical day as games are said to have started up and down the lines with hundreds of men playing, some using a tin can for a ball if they had nothing else. There are reports that in one match that was a little more organised than the rest, a British regiment lost 3-2 to a German one. Whatever the score was, it remains one of the most poignant and wonderful moments in history.

DECEMBER 26

The best and worst of two Scousers, both England strikers, was on display on this day. In 2001, landlord and purveyor of comedy goal celebrations Robbie Fowler was hitting his old heights when, little over a month after leaving boyhood club Liverpool for Leeds United for £11m, he scored a hat-trick in a 3-0 win at Bolton.

A year to the day later, and fellow Merseyside front-man Wayne Rooney was showing his fiery side when he received the first red card of his career. The hot-headed young striker was sent off for a late challenge on Steve Vickers in a 1-1 draw between Birmingham and Everton. It was the first sign that along with his prodigious talent, Rooney had the dodgy temperament to match.

DECEMBER 27

David Dunn was at one time being touted by Blackburn fans and the typically over-excited tabloids as being 'the new Gazza'. The Blackburn Rovers midfielder, born today in 1979, made a name for himself as the fulcrum of the free-flowing Blackburn Rovers side that won promotion to the Premiership in 2001. His flair and ability on the ball led to comparisons with Gascoigne but he was never really the successor to Gazza and in the end he won just one England cap, when he played against Portugal in a friendly at Villa Park in 2002.

In contrast to Dunn, Tom Crawshaw, who was born today in 1872, was a tough centre-half who captained Sheffield Wednesday to two league titles and two FA Cup wins between 1896 and 1907. He was capped ten times by England and scored one goal.

DECEMBER 28

The footballing allegiances of the Beatles has long been debated among fans: were they Blues or Reds? Some claim they must have preferred Anfield to Goodison, pointing to the fact that on the cover of the Sergeant Pepper's Lonely Hearts Club Band album, the only footballer pictured is a Liverpool player. That man is Albert Stubbins, a former Newcastle United centre forward who was a prolific poacher for both the Magpies and Liverpool. He played just once for England in a wartime international match against Wales at West Brom. He failed to score as the Welsh won 1-0 and he never played again for England. Stubbins passed away on this day in 2002 aged 82.

In 2008 former England captain Terry Butcher, who was born today in 1958, said he would never get over Maradona's 'Hand of God'. 'I'll never forgive him. I felt it more than anybody else,' said Scotland assistant manager Butcher in 2008 before a match against Maradona's Argentina. Maradona had the last laugh though; when asked about Butcher's views he replied: 'Who is Butcher?'

DECEMBER 29

The England/Germany rivalry was played out in microcosm today in 2003 in a Southampton versus Arsenal clash by some-time England striker Kevin Phillips and Germany goalkeeper Jens Lehmann. Famous for his childish behaviour on the pitch, Lehmann lost his rag with Phillips who he claimed had stepped on his foot. As the diminutive striker walked away Lehmann flung the ball at the back of his head. The referee intervened and amid cries of 'he started it!' told them to pack it in and get on with the game.

Kieron Dyer has also been known to show some petulant behaviour on the football field. The injury-prone midfielder, capped 28 times by England, was born on this day in 1978.

DECEMBER 30

Christmas time may be pantomime season and Scottish referee Dougie Smith deserved all the boos and hisses he got today in 1995 for one of the meanest pieces of over-zealous refereeing ever seen on a football pitch. With Rangers in the middle of a 7-0 win over Hibs at Ibrox, Paul Gascoigne noticed that Smith had dropped his cards and pen on the turf. Gazza picked them up and showed the ref his own yellow card, much to the delight of the 44,692 crowd who cheered his cheeky gesture. The ref did not find it funny at all and as soon as Gazza had given him the card back he promptly showed it to the midfielder for dissent. 'He might be able to take the f**king piss out of you, but he's not taking the f**king piss out of me,' Smith told Hibs midfielder Joe Tortolano who had asked him why he was being such a Scrooge.

He made perhaps the greatest save ever, and was one of England's best ever players. Gordon Banks was born on this day in 1937, was in goal for England's World Cup win in 1966 and made the unbelievable save from a Pele header in the 1970 tournament. Had he not been struck down with a bout of food poisoning the night before England's quarter-final match with West Germany, many believe England could have defended their trophy successfully.

DECEMBER 31

When former England skipper Alan Shearer finally took over as Newcastle manager in April 2009 it came after nearly a decade of hints and assumptions that he would one day take the job. Today in 2000 the *Sunday Mirror* published an article, in which Shearer was quoted, claiming that the number nine would take over from then manager Sir Bobby Robson in the summer of 2002. Just like every other rumour about his impending employment in the role until 2009, it never came to fruition. Former England boss Sir Bobby carried on until 2004 while Shearer continued playing until 2006.

If the blame for Steve McClaren being inflicted on England fans can be laid at one man's door, it is Brian Barwick. The former head of sport for the BBC and ITV was chief executive of the Football Association from 2005 until today in 2008 when he stepped down from his role. 'I am sad to be leaving the FA – an organisation it has been a privilege to lead – but I believe it is in the best interests of all parties,' said Barwick in a statement. 'I have always endeavoured to do my job with passion, decency and integrity, and I believe I am leaving a strong legacy for the future.'

Also available at all good book stores

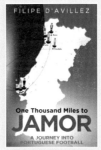

9781785316258

9781785316326

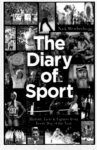

9781785316289

9781785316449

9781785316869

9781785316463